Great Taste ~ Low Fat

HOLIDAY COOKING

TIME
LIFE
BOOKS

ALEXANDRIA, VIRGINIA

TABLE OF CONTENTS

Roast Salmon with Mushroom-Rice Stuffing

Appetizers

Main Courses

Side Dishes

Lemon Champagne Granita

~

page 117

INTRODUCTION

Our mission at Great Taste~Low Fat is to take the work and worry out of everyday low-fat cooking; to provide delicious, fresh, and filling recipes for family and friends; to use quick, streamlined methods and available ingredients; and, within every recipe, to keep the percentage of calories from fat under 30 percent.

HOLIDAY COOKING

The holidays are a time to savor joyful memories and to create new holiday traditions with family and friends. And what better way to celebrate than to share glorious food—everything from roast turkey to a plate of oven-warm cookies. But for many of us during the holidays, stress can be an unwelcome guest. There's not enough time to prepare all the food we'd like: cookies, cakes, food gifts to give, endless side dishes, and on and on. And most traditional recipes are full of diet-busting fat and calories.

But not to worry. *Holiday Cooking* will help you through it all with style. Consider this volume a cook, party-planner, and personal shopper, all wrapped in one package. Remember, too, these recipes and ideas work for any special occasion or festive gathering—this is a book for all seasons.

Our chefs have tackled the dilemma of holiday feasting, and have created a holiday miracle: recipes that capture all the flavor and texture of the classic favorites while keeping the calories from fat under 30 percent. The recipes are easy to follow and incorporate all the principles of low-fat cooking: the judicious use of fats, and a reliance on reduced-fat dairy products and highly flavored ingredients.

COMPLETE HOLIDAY GUIDE

Our book begins, logically enough, with Appetizers. Here you'll find fancy "finger foods," including canapé toasts topped with smoked salmon and delectable, bite-size cheese puffs. If you require an enticing first course, our samples range from Waldorf salad to a brandy-laced shrimp bisque.

The next chapter is Main Courses, which stars roast turkey, naturally, with a host of stuffings, from savory oyster to classic corn bread. For the nontraditionalist, there is roast loin of pork with a currant glaze, and a spectacular roast salmon fillet with a wild mushroom stuffing. Side Dishes offers low-fat versions of all-time holiday favorites—creamy corn pudding and garlic mashed potatoes, as well as tastefully intriguing combinations such as apples poached in herbed cranberry juice.

In Desserts, you'll find a full selection of scrumptious treats. They include a chocolaty-rich bread pudding, shortcakes with a pear-cranberry sauce, an elegant Champagne granita, and, of course, a pumpkin pie. Finally, the Homemade Gifts chapter has something for everyone on your list: chocolate truffles, a decadent butterscotch sauce, delicious quick breads, and more. Best of all, many of these gifts can be started weeks or even months ahead for stress-free giving during the season.

To tailor this volume to the specific demands of entertaining at holiday time, we've introduced some new features. "Suggested Accompaniments" in the other books has become "Helpful Hints," with make-ahead tips, ingredient substitutions, and suggestions for using leftovers. The nutritional values are calculated for easier meal planning: Where appropriate, rather than presuming a serving size, we give the total yield, and the nutrition is for measured quantities, such as ½ cup of a side dish or a per-piece value, as with cookies.

To help you organize your time in the kitchen, the "working times" for our recipes give a realistic idea of how long you'll spend doing hands-on tasks. The "total times" include chilling, cooking, and advance preparation, making it easy for you to plan. Finally, our "Secrets of Low-Fat Holiday Cooking" section offers practical help for getting through the holidays: menu planning (including sample menus); a guide to stuffing and trussing a turkey; how to make low-fat gravy; and the ins and outs of home canning. There are also low-fat ideas for using turkey leftovers.

This holiday season, step aside and invite our chefs into your home. Simple recipes, guaranteeing great results, will make the holidays a time of pleasure for everyone—especially the cook.

CONTRIBUTING EDITORS

Sandra Rose Gluck, a New York City chef, has years of experience creating delicious low-fat recipes that are quick to prepare. Her secret for satisfying results is to always aim for great taste and variety. By combining readily available, fresh ingredients with simple cooking techniques, Sandra has created the perfect recipes for today's busy lifestyles.

Grace Young has been the director of a major test kitchen specializing in low-fat and health-related cookbooks for over 12 years. Grace oversees the development, taste testing, and nutritional analysis of every recipe in Great Taste-Low Fat. Her goal is simple: take the work and worry out of low-fat cooking so that you can enjoy delicious, healthy meals every day.

Kate Slate has been a food editor for almost 20 years, and has published thousands of recipes in cookbooks and magazines. As the Editorial Director of Great Taste-Low Fat, Kate combined simple, easy to follow directions with practical low-fat cooking tips. The result is guaranteed to make your low-fat cooking as rewarding and fun as it is foolproof.

NUTRITION

Every recipe in *Great Taste-Low Fat* provides per-serving values for the nutrients listed in the chart at right. The daily intakes listed in the chart are based on those recommended by the USDA and presume a nonsedentary lifestyle. The nutritional emphasis in this book is not only on controlling calories, but on reducing total fat grams. Research has shown that dietary fat metabolizes more easily into body fat than do carbohydrates and protein. In order to control the amount of fat in a given recipe and in your diet in general, no more than 30 percent of the calories should come from fat.

Nutrient	Women	Men
Fat	<65 g	<80 g
Calories	2000	2500
Saturated fat	<20 g	<25 g
Carbohydrate	300 g	375 g
Protein	50 g	65 g
Cholesterol	<300 mg	<300 mg
Sodium	<2400 mg	<2400 mg

These recommended daily intakes are averages used by the Food and Drug Administration and are consistent with the labeling on all food products. Although the values for cholesterol and sodium are the same for all adults, the other intake values vary depending on gender, ideal weight, and activity level. Check with a physician or nutritionist for your own daily intake values.

SECRETS OF LOW-FAT HOLIDAY COOKING

HOLIDAY COOKING

Holiday time comes but once a year, but, oh, what a time! There are so many occasions to celebrate with family and friends—from festive dinners and magnificent buffets to cozy, laughter-filled parties. Use this volume as a reference for all your holiday cooking, or just pick and choose to supplement your own traditional favorites.

In "Secrets of Low-Fat Holiday Cooking," we've set forth a sumptuous feast for twelve plus a handy countdown for getting it all on the table, as well as several other sample menus. We also provide instructions for stuffing and trussing a turkey and for preparing low-fat gravy; recipe suggestions for turkey leftovers; and a "how-to" section on making homemade gifts in jars. After the holidays, don't relegate this book to the back of the shelf. Anytime there's an occasion to celebrate—birthday, anniversary, or just the beginning of spring—turn to these pages of splendid food.

MENU PLANNING

Just a little organization will turn the ambitious meals typical of holiday entertaining into manageable cook's play. Start with the obvious—select the dishes that will make up your menu. Do keep in mind that the more guests at the gathering, the more courses or dishes you'll probably need (which translates into smaller servings since there will be more variety). Use our "Old-Fashioned Feast for Twelve" as an easy-to-follow model for planning your recipe preparation.

OLD-FASHIONED FEAST FOR TWELVE

The Appetizers
Miniature Cheese Puffs • Spinach Turnovers
• Festive Open-Face Sandwiches

The Main Course
Stuffed Roast Turkey • Herbed
Corn Bread Stuffing • Cranberry Sauce

The Side Dishes
Green Beans and Toasted Almonds
• Orange-Glazed Carrots • Shallot-Topped Garlic
Mashed Potatoes • Spoonbread • Angel Biscuits

The Desserts
Pumpkin Chiffon Pie with Pecans
• Deep-Dish Apple Cobbler

• **Well in advance:** Prepare spinach turnovers and freeze. Make cranberry sauce and refrigerate.

• **The day before:** Make pumpkin pie and refrigerate. Make corn bread for stuffing and hold at room temperature. Make glazed carrots (without scallion garnish) and refrigerate. Make herbed cheese for open-face sandwiches and refrigerate. Make cheese puffs and hold at room temperature.

• **The morning of:** Prepare corn bread stuffing and refrigerate. Prepare crust and filling separately for apple cobbler and refrigerate. Prepare green beans (without almond garnish) and refrigerate. Prepare angel biscuits and hold at room temperature. Stuff and roast the turkey.

• **An hour before serving:** Prepare mashed potatoes. Bake dish of corn bread stuffing. Prepare and bake spoonbread. Bake spinach turnovers. Reheat cheese puffs. Reheat angel biscuits. Assemble apple cobbler and bake.

• **At the last minute:** Assemble open-face sandwiches. Reheat glazed carrots and add garnish. Reheat green beans and add garnish.

SAMPLE MENUS

We all have our tried-and-true favorites for holiday dining. But in case you'd like a few more ideas to help you through the season, we offer on the next page a few sample menus—from casual and family style to intimate and elegant.

GLORIOUS HOLIDAY FEAST
For 8

~

Spinach Turnovers

Smoked Salmon Toasts

•

Turkey Breast with Wild Rice
Stuffing

Cranberry Sauce

Bourbon-Glazed Yams

Creamed Spinach with Red Bell
Pepper

Shallot-Topped Garlic Mashed
Potatoes

Potato Icebox Rolls

•

Chocolate Angel Food Cake with
Raspberry Glaze

Chocolate-Dipped Fruits

HOME-STYLE ROAST
CHICKEN DINNER
For 4

~

Mushroom-Filled Phyllo Shells

•

Roast Chicken with Classic Bread Stuffing

Green Beans and Toasted Almonds

Roasted Winter Vegetables

Potato Pancakes with Applesauce

•

Holiday Honey Cake

Hazelnut Macaroons

WARM WINTER DINNER
For 6

~

Brandied Shrimp Bisque

•

Currant-Glazed Pork with Sweet Potato
Purée

Brussels Sprouts with Chestnuts

Cranberry-Poached Herbed Apples

•

Gingerbread with Lemon Sauce

ELEGANT NEW YEAR'S
EVE SUPPER
For 4

~

Oyster Stew

Caviar-Stuffed Endive Leaves

•

Roast Salmon with
Mushroom-Rice Stuffing

Minted Peas and Pearl Onions

•

Lemon Champagne Granita

Fallen Chocolate Mousse Cake

For safety, always stuff the turkey just before roasting—no sooner—and then roast it immediately. Promptly remove all the stuffing from the cavities of the cooked turkey. Fresh turkeys are more flavorful than frozen, and should be cooked within 2 days of purchase. If you do use a frozen bird, thaw it in the refrigerator, not on the kitchen counter, allowing 24 hours for each 5 pounds of turkey. We recommend not buying a pre-basted turkey, which may contain added fat. Trussing keeps the stuffing in the turkey and also helps it hold its shape during roasting for a neater presentation.

Stuffing a Turkey

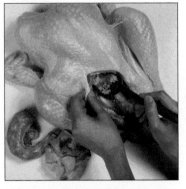

After removing the giblets, rinse the turkey with cold water, pat it dry, and then spoon the stuffing loosely into the body cavity. Stuffing needs room to expand during cooking.

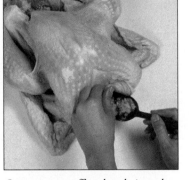

Spoon more stuffing loosely into the neck cavity. Extra stuffing can be placed in a baking dish, covered with foil, and baked with the turkey for the last 30 minutes of roasting.

Trussing a Turkey

To close the turkey body cavity, slide several bamboo skewers (each cut in half) through the skin. Bring the neck skin over the stuffing, and then fold the wing tips under the bird.

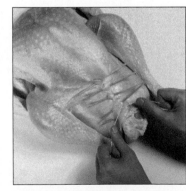

Starting at the skewer at the top of the cavity opening, loop a long string around the skewers. Cross the string and lace back and forth; pull tightly to firmly close the two flaps of skin.

Wrap the ends of the string several times around the ends of the turkey legs to hold them snugly in place against the bird. Knot the string to secure.

Making Gravy

Once the turkey is roasted, you will have delicious drippings and browned bits in the roasting pan, which can be turned into either a flour-thickened gravy or a natural juice version. While the turkey is roasting, prepare 2 cups of giblet broth (p. 37). Alternatively, use 2 cups of defatted reduced-sodium canned chicken broth. While the turkey is standing, pour off the fat from the roasting pan. Place the pan over medium heat and pour in the giblet or canned broth, scraping up the browned bits with a gravy whisk or wooden spoon.

For a flour-thickened gravy, place 2 tablespoons of flour in a saucepan, and gradually whisk in ¼ cup of the broth mixture until smooth. Then whisk in the remaining broth mixture. Cook, whisking, until the gravy is thickened, about 5 minutes. For a natural juice gravy, omit the flour step and simply cook the broth mixture in the roasting pan over medium-high heat until reduced and flavorful.

USING LEFTOVERS

One of the benefits of holiday cooking is a bounty of leftovers, especially when it comes to the big bird. If you still have the stamina after the table has been cleared, remove the meat from the leftover legs, wings, rib cage, and any other parts. If someone in the family has a preference for dark or white meat, you may want to package the meat separately in sturdy plastic bags or aluminum foil packets. And by all means, don't toss out that carcass—it's the beginning of a wonderful homemade broth. You should plan to use any leftover turkey within 3 to 4 days at the most.

Our chefs have provided the following recipes as guidelines—you can easily add or subtract ingredients to suit your own taste, since these are the kinds of dishes that welcome the cook's personal touch. Figure on each recipe serving 4 to 5.

Turkey Soup

The critical beginning for any homemade soup is the broth—this takes no effort and can be prepared a day or two ahead. Place the turkey carcass in a large pot (cut it up if it doesn't quite fit). Add enough cold water to cover. Add a cut-up carrot or two, some cut-up celery, a quartered onion, a bay leaf, and some black peppercorns. Cover the pot and let it simmer for a couple of hours—your kitchen will be heavenly with rich aromas. Strain the broth and discard the solids. If time permits, chill the broth overnight—the fat will rise to the top for easy removal. If not, ladle the top layer of the broth into a gravy separator and pour off the fat. Return the broth to a clean pot. Bring to a simmer, add 3 cups of cut-up "hard" vegetables (carrots, white potatoes, turnips, parsnips), and cook until tender. Then add 2 cups of "semi-hard" vegetables (bell peppers, green beans, leeks) and cook until crisp-tender. Season with salt, black pepper, and perhaps some thyme or rosemary. For a final flourish, add 2 cups of diced cooked turkey along with vegetables that require practically no cooking—frozen peas or corn, and chopped fresh tomatoes—and warm through.

Turkey Shepherd's Pie

Savory supper pies are the perfect culinary canvas for exercising your creative urges with leftovers. Measure about 4 cups of leftover cooked turkey and vegetables, which is enough to fill a 9-inch deep-dish pie plate, plus 2 to 3 cups of leftover mashed white or sweet potatoes, or a mixture. To bind the filling ingredients together, prepare a simple white sauce: Place 3 tablespoons flour in a medium saucepan, and gradually whisk in 1½ cups low-fat (1%) milk over medium heat. Bring to a boil and cook, whisking frequently, until the mixture is slightly thickened, about 4 minutes. Season the sauce with salt and black pepper and other herbs and spices that will enhance the flavors of the leftovers. Combine the white sauce with the turkey and vegetables, spoon into the pie plate, and top with the potatoes, either forming a ring around the edge or covering the entire top. Place the pie on a baking sheet and bake in a preheated 350° oven until the filling is bubbly and the potatoes are lightly golden, about 20 minutes.

Turkey Salad

Start with 2 to 3 cups of diced cooked turkey. Toss in 2 ribs celery, sliced, 1 red or green bell pepper, diced, 1 pear or apple, cored and diced, and 1 leftover sweet potato, peeled and diced. For a low-fat dressing, mix ½ cup plain nonfat yogurt, ¼ cup reduced-sodium chicken broth, 2 tablespoons reduced-fat mayonnaise, 1 tablespoon Dijon mustard, 1 tablespoon fresh lemon juice, ½ teaspoon salt, and ¼ teaspoon black pepper. Vary the dressing by adding ¾ teaspoon of seasoning from an ethnic cuisine: Make it Mexican with cumin; Indian with curry powder; French with dried tarragon; and Italian with dried oregano.

GIFTS IN JARS

Homemade condiments are always appreciated. For extended shelf storage, process foods such as pickled vegetables, jellies, or chutneys in a boiling water bath to destroy harmful bacteria. The amount of time required for processing depends on the acidity and density of the food as well as the size of the canning container. We indicate in the recipes both the container size and timing.

To prepare for canning, wash empty glass canning jars and screw bands and lids in hot soapy water and rinse well. Keep the lids and bands in hot water. To sterilize, place the empty jars, right-side up, on the rack in a water bath canner, cover with hot water by 1 inch, then boil for 10 minutes. Drain. Transfer the food to the sterilized jars, leaving the recommended amount of headspace. (Always place hot food in hot jars.) If you are reusing screw band jars or clamp jars, be sure the gasket pieces are new or the seals will not work. Carefully place the jars back onto the canning rack, and follow the directions in the captions at right.

Once processed, check the seals. If using the two-piece metal canning tops, remove the screw bands after the jars have cooled. Press the middle of the lid; if the lid pops up when you release your finger, the jar is not sealed and must be re-processed. To test jars with glass tops and wire fasteners, tip the jars when fully cooled; there should be no leaking. Label each gift with what's in the jar, when it was made, and how to store it once it's been opened. Properly processed, sealed jars will keep in a cool, dry, dark area for up to one year.

Water Bath Canning

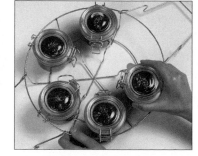

Spoon the food into a sterilized jar, using a sterilized funnel and leaving a small amount of headspace, which will vary according to the food being processed. Remove air bubbles by running a plastic spatula around the inside of the jar. Wipe the rim with a clean damp cloth for a good seal, then cover with the top.

Fill a water bath canner half full with very hot water. Place the sealed jars on the canning rack and lower into the pot, making sure the jars do not touch. Add enough boiling water to come 1 inch above the tops of the jars. Turn the heat to the highest setting until the water boils vigorously. Process according to the recipe.

To remove the jars from the water bath, carefully lift the rack with oven mitts, using the handles. If you don't have such a rack, use special jar-holding tongs, or even oven mitts, although the mitts will be more difficult to maneuver. Let the jars cool completely on a rack, and then check the seals (see "Gifts in Jars," at left).

APPETIZERS

1

GOLDEN BUTTERNUT-APPLE SOUP

MAKES: 6 CUPS
WORKING TIME: 25 MINUTES
TOTAL TIME: 30 MINUTES

3 cups peeled, seeded, and cut butternut squash (2-inch chunks)

2 Granny Smith apples, peeled, cored, and cut into 1-inch chunks

1 medium onion, coarsely chopped

2 cups reduced-sodium chicken broth, defatted

2 tablespoons firmly packed dark brown sugar

½ teaspoon ground ginger

¼ teaspoon cinnamon

½ cup low-fat (1%) milk

2 tablespoons dark rum

¼ cup reduced-fat sour cream

2 scallions, thinly sliced on the diagonal

1. In a Dutch oven, combine the squash, apples, onion, broth, brown sugar, ginger, and cinnamon. Cover and cook over medium-high heat, stirring occasionally, until the squash is very tender, about 10 minutes.

2. With a slotted spoon, transfer the solids to a blender or food processor and purée until smooth. Return the purée to the pan, add the milk and rum, and stir well to combine. Cook over low heat, uncovered, until the soup is just heated through, about 3 minutes.

3. Ladle the soup into bowls and spoon 2 or 3 small dollops of the sour cream on top of each. With a skewer or knife, cut through the sour cream to form a decorative pattern. Sprinkle the scallions on top and serve.

Helpful hints: Prepare the squash purée up to 2 days ahead, refrigerate, and then stir in the milk and rum just before serving and gently heat. If desired, cook the squash mixture in the microwave: Combine the ingredients in step 1 in a microwave-safe bowl, and microwave on high power for 10 to 15 minutes, stirring halfway through.

VALUES ARE PER 1 CUP
FAT: 2G/13%
CALORIES: 128
SATURATED FAT: 0.8G
CARBOHYDRATE: 24G
PROTEIN: 4G
CHOLESTEROL: 4MG
SODIUM: 231MG

Set your holiday table with candlelight, and present this colorful soup as a festive first course. It's guaranteed to spark appetites—tart apples and a hint of rum delicately sweeten the squash, while ginger and cinnamon lend an invitingly spicy scent. Ladle into pottery soup bowls, or into heavy mugs for a more casual gathering around the fire.

PEAR AND ROQUEFORT SALAD

SERVES: 4
WORKING TIME: 20 MINUTES
TOTAL TIME: 20 MINUTES

1 cup canned pear nectar

2 tablespoons fresh lime juice

1 tablespoon honey

1 teaspoon minced fresh ginger

¼ teaspoon salt

¼ teaspoon freshly ground black pepper

4 Bartlett pears, cored and thinly sliced lengthwise

2 bunches watercress, thick stems trimmed

½ cup dried currants

2 ounces Roquefort cheese, crumbled (about ¼ cup)

2 tablespoons coarsely chopped pecans, toasted

1. In a large bowl, combine the nectar, lime juice, honey, ginger, salt, and pepper and stir to blend. Add the pears and toss well to coat.

2. Place the watercress on 4 salad plates, arrange the pears on top, and spoon any remaining dressing over. Garnish with the currants, Roquefort, and pecans and serve.

Helpful hints: You can toss the pear slices with the dressing earlier in the day and refrigerate, and then assemble the salads just before serving. If good-quality watercress is unavailable, substitute shredded romaine lettuce or curly endive.

The classic winter flavors of sweetly ripe pears and pungent Roquefort are nicely enhanced by peppery watercress and toasted pecans. Arrange the salads on individual plates, fanning the pear slices over the watercress, and offer them as a first course for roasted chicken or baked ham.

FAT: 7G/23%
CALORIES: 289
SATURATED FAT: 3G
CARBOHYDRATE: 55G
PROTEIN: 7G
CHOLESTEROL: 13MG
SODIUM: 431MG

These whimsical, melt-in-the-mouth pastry shells explode with a rich mushroom and basil flavor. This appetizer makes an enticing display on a tray for a holiday buffet or open house—but do include knives and forks for the crumbly shells rather than serving them as finger food. Basil leaves and halved cherry tomatoes make a nice garnish.

MUSHROOM-FILLED PHYLLO SHELLS

MAKES: 1 DOZEN
WORKING TIME: 30 MINUTES
TOTAL TIME: 50 MINUTES

*Four 17 x 11-inch sheets phyllo
dough, thawed if frozen*

*½ cup reduced-sodium chicken
broth, defatted*

1 tablespoon minced shallots

1 clove garlic, minced

*½ pound fresh mushrooms
(button, shiitake, cremini, or a
mixture), coarsely chopped*

½ cup finely diced carrot

¼ cup dry white wine

2 tablespoons chopped fresh basil

*¼ teaspoon freshly ground black
pepper*

1. Preheat the oven to 325°. Lightly spray a 12-cup miniature muffin
   pan with nonstick cooking spray.

2. Lightly spray 1 phyllo sheet with nonstick cooking spray. Stack the
   remaining phyllo sheets on top, lightly spraying each sheet with
   nonstick cooking spray. Cut the stack into 12 rectangles (see tip; top
   photo). Place 1 rectangle stack in each prepared muffin cup, pressing gently into the bottom to form a shell (bottom photo). Bake
   for 8 to 10 minutes, or until the phyllo is lightly golden. Carefully
   remove the shells from the pan and transfer to a wire rack to cool.

3. Meanwhile, in a medium saucepan, combine ¼ cup of the broth,
   the shallots, and garlic. Bring to a boil, reduce to a simmer, and
   cook until the liquid has evaporated, about 3 minutes. Stir in the
   mushrooms, carrot, wine, and remaining ¼ cup broth. Return to
   a boil over medium heat and cook until the carrot is tender and
   the liquid has evaporated, about 8 minutes longer.

4. Remove the mixture from the heat, stir in the basil and pepper,
   and let cool for 5 minutes. Divide the phyllo shells among plates,
   spoon some mushroom mixture into each shell, and serve.

*Helpful hint: You can prepare the filling 1 day ahead, omitting the basil
and pepper, and chill. To serve, gently reheat the mushroom mixture,
stirring in the basil and pepper at the end for the freshest flavor.*

VALUES ARE PER SHELL
FAT: 0.9G/23%
CALORIES: 34
SATURATED FAT: 0.1G
CARBOHYDRATE: 5G
PROTEIN: 1G
CHOLESTEROL: 0MG
SODIUM: 60MG

TIP

*Working quickly to prevent
the phyllo from drying out,
cut the stacked sheets
of phyllo into 12 rectangles
with a sharp knife. Line
each of the miniature
muffin-pan cups with a
rectangle of phyllo dough,
gently pushing the phyllo
into the pan to form
a shell.*

17

FESTIVE OPEN-FACE SANDWICHES

MAKES: 2 DOZEN
WORKING TIME: 50 MINUTES
TOTAL TIME: 50 MINUTES

8 small shrimp, shelled and deveined

1 ounce reduced-fat cream cheese (Neufchâtel)

¼ cup mixed chopped fresh herbs (parsley, dill, and chives)

2 tablespoons reduced-fat mayonnaise

½ teaspoon grated lemon zest

1 teaspoon fresh lemon juice

¼ teaspoon salt

⅛ teaspoon freshly ground black pepper

24 slices cocktail rye bread

¼ cup thinly sliced cucumber

¼ cup halved cherry tomatoes

¼ cup watercress sprigs, trimmed

¼ cup thinly sliced radishes

1 tablespoon drained capers

1 tablespoon finely chopped green olives

1 tablespoon finely chopped pimiento

1. Heat a medium saucepan of water to boiling over high heat. Add the shrimp and return to a boil. Reduce the heat to medium and cook until the shrimp are just opaque, about 1 minute. Drain, rinse under cold water, and drain again thoroughly. Cut each shrimp in half lengthwise and set aside.

2. In a small bowl, combine the cream cheese, herbs, mayonnaise, lemon zest, lemon juice, salt, and pepper and stir until smooth. Spread the herbed cream cheese over the bread, using about 1 teaspoon of the mixture for each slice.

3. Divide the cucumber, tomatoes, watercress, radishes, and shrimp among the bread, arranging attractively and making a variety of sandwiches. Garnish with the capers, olives, and pimiento. Place the sandwiches on plates and serve.

Helpful hints: The herbed cream cheese can be prepared 1 day ahead, and in fact the flavor will improve. Any leftover spread would be delicious spooned into hollowed-out cherry tomatoes or Belgian endive leaves for an appetizer. For the best appearance, assemble the sandwiches just before serving. If desired, you may substitute flat breads for the rye.

VALUES ARE PER SANDWICH
FAT: 0.8G/26%
CALORIES: 28
SATURATED FAT: 0.3G
CARBOHYDRATE: 4G
PROTEIN: 1G
CHOLESTEROL: 5MG
SODIUM: 106MG

Borrowing from the Scandinavian tradition of entertaining, we've created a pretty potpourri of open-face sandwiches. Their fresh tastes and sprightly flavors are sure to encourage guests to indulge. Although the ingredient list seems long, your choice of toppings is flexible. For instance, if you don't have radishes, just double up on one of the other ingredients.

OYSTER STEW

SERVES: 4
WORKING TIME: 25 MINUTES
TOTAL TIME: 45 MINUTES

*O*ur tasty version of this classic stew, infused with the flavors of the sea, is a delightful beginning to an elegant holiday meal.

3 slices firm-textured white bread, cut into 1-inch squares

1 teaspoon unsalted butter

¼ cup minced shallots or scallion whites

⅔ cup dry white wine

36 oysters, shucked, 1 cup liquor reserved

Bottled clam juice (optional)

1 cup evaporated low-fat milk

½ teaspoon salt

¼ teaspoon freshly ground black pepper

⅛ teaspoon cayenne pepper

2 teaspoons cornstarch mixed with 1 tablespoon water

¼ teaspoon paprika

2 tablespoons chopped fresh parsley

1. Preheat the oven to 400°. Spread the bread on a baking sheet and bake for 5 minutes, or until lightly golden and crisp. Set aside. Meanwhile, in a large saucepan, melt the butter over low heat. Add the shallots and cook, stirring frequently, until the shallots are tender, about 7 minutes. Add the wine, increase the heat to high, and cook until the liquid is reduced by half, about 5 minutes.

2. In a measuring cup, combine the reserved 1 cup oyster liquor (if you don't have enough oyster liquor, add enough clam juice to make 1 cup) and 1 cup of water. Stir the liquor mixture, evaporated milk, salt, black pepper, and cayenne into the shallot mixture and bring to a boil.

3. Stir in the cornstarch mixture and cook, stirring constantly, until the mixture is slightly thickened, about 1 minute. Reduce to a simmer, slip the oysters into the pan, and cook just until the edges are curled, about 3 minutes. Remove from the heat and stir in the paprika. Ladle the oyster stew into 4 bowls, sprinkle the croutons and parsley on top, and serve.

Helpful hints: Since fresh oysters are so delicate, this stew is best served immediately after preparation. On the day you plan to make the stew, have your fishmonger shuck the oysters, reserving the liquor (juice).

FAT: 6G/23%
CALORIES: 234
SATURATED FAT: 1.5G
CARBOHYDRATE: 22G
PROTEIN: 15G
CHOLESTEROL: 83MG
SODIUM: 572MG

SMOKED SALMON TOASTS

MAKES: 1 DOZEN
WORKING TIME: 30 MINUTES
TOTAL TIME: 1 HOUR 30 MINUTES (INCLUDES DRAINING TIME)

1 cup plain nonfat yogurt

3 ounces smoked salmon

2 ounces reduced-fat cream cheese (Neufchâtel)

1 tablespoon snipped fresh dill

1 teaspoon finely chopped shallot

⅛ teaspoon freshly ground black pepper

12 thin slices diagonally cut baguette

2 cloves garlic, halved

12 dill sprigs

1. Line the inside of a sieve with a double thickness of paper towels. Spoon the yogurt into the prepared sieve and set the sieve over a bowl. Let stand at room temperature until the yogurt is thickened and has released its liquid, about 1 hour. Discard the liquid in the bowl.

2. In a food processor, combine the yogurt, 2 ounces of the salmon, the cream cheese, snipped dill, shallot, and pepper. Process until blended but still slightly chunky, using 6 or 7 on/off pulses. Cut the remaining 1 ounce salmon into thin strips and set aside.

3. Preheat the broiler. Rub both sides of the baguette slices with the cut sides of the garlic; discard the garlic. Place the slices on the broiler rack and broil 4 inches from the heat for 2 minutes per side, or until lightly golden and crisp.

4. Spread the salmon-cream cheese mixture over the toasts. Garnish with the reserved salmon strips and the dill sprigs. Place the salmon toasts on a platter and serve.

Helpful hints: The drained yogurt can be used as the basis for any dip or spread that begins with mayonnaise or full-fat sour cream. The salmon-cream cheese mixture can be prepared up to 2 days ahead and refrigerated. This combination is also a tasty topping for toasted bagels for a holiday brunch.

VALUES ARE PER SALMON TOAST
FAT: 2G/26%
CALORIES: 59
SATURATED FAT: 0.8G
CARBOHYDRATE: 7G
PROTEIN: 4G
CHOLESTEROL: 6MG
SODIUM: 147MG

These absolutely heavenly little bites of smoked salmon, cream cheese, and fresh dill will disappear fast.

CREAM OF PUMPKIN SOUP WITH PARMESAN CROUTONS

MAKES: 6 CUPS
WORKING TIME: 20 MINUTES
TOTAL TIME: 45 MINUTES

This tantalizing soup is uniquely seasoned with chili powder, sage, and a dash of vinegar, and richly colored with tomato paste. And the homemade Parmesan croutons add a welcome crunch. This is delightful and soothing as a first course, or serve on its own to your out-of-town company for an afternoon pick-me-up.

2 teaspoons olive oil

1 large onion, sliced

1 clove garlic, sliced

1 sweet potato (about 10 ounces), peeled and thinly sliced

1⅓ cups reduced-sodium chicken broth, defatted

3 tablespoons tomato paste

1¼ teaspoons chili powder

1 teaspoon sugar

¾ teaspoon dried sage

½ teaspoon salt

2 tablespoons grated Parmesan cheese

2 slices firm-textured white bread

2 cups low-fat (1%) milk

2 cups canned solid-pack pumpkin purée

2 tablespoons rice vinegar or cider vinegar

1. In a large saucepan, heat the oil until hot but not smoking over medium heat. Add the onion and garlic and cook, stirring frequently, until the onion is softened, about 7 minutes. Add the sweet potato, stirring to coat. Stir in the broth, 1⅓ cups of water, the tomato paste, chili powder, sugar, sage, and salt and bring to a boil. Reduce to a simmer, cover, and cook until the potato is tender, about 15 minutes.

2. Meanwhile, preheat the oven to 400°. Sprinkle the Parmesan over the bread, place on a baking sheet, and bake for 7 minutes, or until the cheese is lightly browned. Cut the bread into 1-inch squares and set aside.

3. Stir the milk and pumpkin into the sweet potato mixture and return to a boil. Reduce to a simmer and cook, uncovered, stirring frequently, until the flavors have blended, about 3 minutes. Stir in the vinegar. Transfer the mixture to a blender or food processor and purée until smooth. Return the purée to the pan and cook over low heat until the soup is heated through, about 3 minutes. Ladle the soup into bowls, sprinkle the croutons on top, and serve.

Helpful hint: Prepare the sweet potato base several days ahead through step 1 and refrigerate. Just before serving, stir in the milk, pumpkin, and vinegar and cook until heated through.

VALUES ARE PER 1 CUP
FAT: 4G/20%
CALORIES: 162
SATURATED FAT: 1.2G
CARBOHYDRATE: 27G
PROTEIN: 7G
CHOLESTEROL: 5MG
SODIUM: 514MG

SHRIMP COCKTAIL

SERVES: 4
WORKING TIME: 20 MINUTES
TOTAL TIME: 50 MINUTES (INCLUDES CHILLING TIME)

A perennial holiday favorite, this simple first course will make your guests feel very cared for. Here tradition is given a zesty contemporary twist as fragrant cilantro and cumin enliven the cocktail sauce. For an attractive presentation, leave the tails on the shrimp, and garnish with lime slices and cilantro sprigs.

¾ pound medium shrimp, shelled and deveined

½ cup chili sauce

2 tablespoons finely chopped fresh cilantro

1 tablespoon fresh lime juice

1½ teaspoons prepared white horseradish

½ teaspoon ground cumin

1 lime, thinly sliced

1. Heat a medium saucepan of water to boiling over high heat. Add the shrimp and return to a boil. Reduce the heat to medium and cook until the shrimp are just opaque, about 2 minutes. Drain, rinse under cold water, and drain again thoroughly.

2. Meanwhile, in a small bowl, combine the chili sauce, cilantro, lime juice, horseradish, and cumin and stir to blend. Transfer the shrimp to a medium bowl. Cover the shrimp and sauce and refrigerate until well chilled, about 30 minutes.

3. Divide the shrimp among 4 plates and serve with the sauce and lime slices.

Helpful hints: Both the shrimp and sauce can be prepared up to 1 day ahead and chilled. For a larger crowd, just multiply the recipe by the appropriate amount and arrange the shrimp on a serving platter or tray. Leftover cocktail sauce perks up roasted beef or poultry.

FAT: 1G/11%
CALORIES: 117
SATURATED FAT: 0.2G
CARBOHYDRATE: 11G
PROTEIN: 15G
CHOLESTEROL: 105MG
SODIUM: 562MG

CAVIAR-STUFFED ENDIVE LEAVES

MAKES: 2 DOZEN
WORKING TIME: 30 MINUTES
TOTAL TIME: 30 MINUTES

½ cup low-fat (1%) cottage cheese

3 tablespoons finely snipped fresh chives or minced scallions

3 Belgian endives, separated into 24 leaves

2 tablespoons salmon caviar

⅓ cup assorted julienned vegetables (red bell pepper, carrot, and scallion)

1. In a mini-food processor or with a hand-held blender, purée the cottage cheese until smooth and creamy. Stir in 2 tablespoons of the chives.

2. Spread a little of the cottage cheese mixture in the base of each endive leaf, then top each mound of cheese with a dab of the caviar. Arrange the vegetables decoratively in the endive leaves. Garnish with the remaining 1 tablespoon chives, place on a platter, and serve.

Helpful hint: To save time, fill the endive leaves and decorate up to 2 hours before serving, omitting the salmon caviar and garnish. Keep refrigerated until ready to serve. Spoon on the caviar and garnish at the last minute, since any sooner and the caviar may "bleed" into the cottage cheese.

VALUES ARE PER STUFFED ENDIVE LEAF
FAT: 0.3G/29%
CALORIES: 8
SATURATED FAT: 0G
CARBOHYDRATE: 0G
PROTEIN: 1G
CHOLESTEROL: 8MG
SODIUM: 40MG

Just the tiniest dollop of salmon caviar makes these endive leaves special enough for the fanciest parties. And these hors d'oeuvres are everything you need to whet the appetite—they're crunchy, creamy, and savory all at once. Depending on your artistic temperament, be as simple or as elaborate as you wish in arranging the julienned vegetables and caviar.

BRANDIED SHRIMP BISQUE

The murmurs of pleasure when your guests taste their first spoonful of this bisque will be reward enough for your effort. Sautéing the shrimp shells with brandy creates an intense shrimp taste, and both carrot juice and tomato-vegetable juice add subtle flavor accents. Serve elegantly in a cup and saucer, with toast points alongside.

2½ teaspoons olive oil

2 pounds medium shrimp, shelled and deveined, shells rinsed, dried, and reserved

1 clove garlic, crushed and peeled

2 tablespoons brandy

2 cups reduced-sodium tomato-vegetable juice

1 cup carrot juice

1 medium onion, sliced

1 teaspoon salt

½ teaspoon dried thyme

¼ teaspoon cayenne pepper

¼ teaspoon freshly ground black pepper

½ cup evaporated low-fat milk

2 teaspoons cornstarch mixed with 1 tablespoon water

¼ cup snipped fresh chives or minced scallions

1. In a nonstick Dutch oven, heat 2 teaspoons of the oil until hot but not smoking over medium heat. Add the shrimp shells and garlic and cook, stirring frequently, until the shells turn red, about 4 minutes. Add the brandy and cook for 1 minute. Stir in the tomato-vegetable juice, carrot juice, 2½ cups of water, the onion, salt, thyme, cayenne, and pepper. Bring to a boil, reduce to a simmer, cover, and cook until the flavors have blended, about 20 minutes. Strain the broth through a fine sieve into a large bowl, pressing on the shells to extract the liquid. Discard the solids; set the broth aside.

2. In a large nonstick skillet, heat the remaining ½ teaspoon oil until hot but not smoking over medium heat. Add the shrimp and cook, stirring frequently, until the shrimp are just opaque, about 4 minutes. Remove 18 shrimp, set aside. Pour the reserved broth over the shrimp in the pan, bring to a boil, and cook until the flavors have blended, about 5 minutes. Transfer the mixture to a food processor (or a blender, in batches) and purée until smooth. Return the purée to the pan, stir in the evaporated milk, and return to a boil.

3. Stir in the cornstarch mixture and cook, stirring constantly, until the mixture is slightly thickened, about 1 minute. Ladle the bisque into 6 bowls, garnish with the reserved shrimp, sprinkle the chives on top, and serve.

FAT: 5G/18%
CALORIES: 227
SATURATED FAT: 0.7G
CARBOHYDRATE: 14G
PROTEIN: 28G
CHOLESTEROL: 190MG
SODIUM: 690MG

*T*hese turnovers are perfect hot hors d'oeuvres for a hungry crowd. The delicious cream cheese pastry—deceptively low in fat—is filled with a robustly flavored spinach and roasted red pepper combination. Serve hot out of the oven or at room temperature with mulled cider, and with a small crock of spicy mustard for dipping.

Spinach Turnovers

MAKES: 3 DOZEN
WORKING TIME: 30 MINUTES
TOTAL TIME: 50 MINUTES

⅓ cup thawed frozen chopped spinach, drained and squeezed dry

¼ cup low-fat (1%) cottage cheese

¼ cup diced jarred roasted red pepper, rinsed and drained

¼ cup chopped fresh basil

2½ teaspoons Dijon mustard

1 teaspoon salt

3½ cups flour

2 tablespoons sugar

2 teaspoons baking powder

1 teaspoon dried marjoram or oregano

2 ounces reduced-fat cream cheese (Neufchâtel)

3 tablespoons unsalted butter

⅔ cup plain nonfat yogurt

¼ cup reduced-fat sour cream

1. In a medium bowl, combine the spinach, cottage cheese, roasted pepper, 2 tablespoons of the basil, ½ teaspoon of the mustard, and ¼ teaspoon of the salt and stir to blend. Set aside.

2. In a large bowl, combine the flour, sugar, baking powder, marjoram, and remaining ¾ teaspoon salt. With a pastry blender or 2 knives, cut in the cream cheese and butter until the mixture resembles coarse meal. Stir in the yogurt, sour cream, remaining 2 tablespoons basil, remaining 2 teaspoons mustard, and about ⅓ cup of cold water just until the dough comes together.

3. Preheat the oven to 400°. On a lightly floured board, roll the dough into a rectangle about ¼ inch thick. With a 3-inch biscuit cutter, cut out about 36 rounds. Spoon 1 teaspoon of the spinach mixture onto half of each round to within ¼ inch of the edges. Brush the edges of 1 round with water, fold in half to enclose the filling and, with a fork, crimp the edges to seal (see tip; top photo). Prick the top (bottom photo) and repeat with the remaining rounds. Transfer to 2 baking sheets and bake for 17 minutes, or until the turnovers are lightly golden.

Helpful hint: The turnovers can be prepared ahead and frozen, unbaked, for up to 1 month. Bake as directed (do not thaw), allowing a few more minutes in the oven.

VALUES ARE PER TURNOVER
FAT: 2G/21%
CALORIES: 69
SATURATED FAT: 1G
CARBOHYDRATE: 11G
PROTEIN: 2G
CHOLESTEROL: 4MG
SODIUM: 117MG

TIP

After brushing the edges of the dough with water, fold half of the dough over the filling, and crimp the edges with a fork to seal. Prick the turnover tops with the fork to allow steam to escape during baking—this keeps the pastry drier and prevents the turnovers from breaking open.

WALDORF SALAD

SERVES: 4
WORKING TIME: 20 MINUTES
TOTAL TIME: 20 MINUTES

1 cup plain nonfat yogurt

2 tablespoons reduced-fat sour cream

2 tablespoons reduced-fat mayonnaise

1 teaspoon grated lemon zest

2 tablespoons fresh lemon juice

¼ teaspoon salt

¼ teaspoon freshly ground black pepper

2 Granny Smith apples, cored and cut into 1-inch chunks

1 Red Delicious apple, cored and cut into 1-inch chunks

2 ribs celery, thinly sliced

1 cup red seedless grapes, halved

1 small head romaine lettuce, cut crosswise into ¼-inch-wide shreds

1 tablespoon coarsely chopped walnuts

1. In a large bowl, combine the yogurt, sour cream, mayonnaise, lemon zest, lemon juice, salt, and pepper and stir to blend. Add the apples, celery, and grapes and toss well to coat.

2. Place the lettuce on 4 salad plates and spoon the apple mixture on top. Garnish with the walnuts and serve.

Helpful hint: To get a jump on the party, toss the apple mixture with the dressing earlier in the day and refrigerate. Just before serving, spoon over the shredded lettuce and then garnish with the walnuts.

Everyone will recognize this favorite, but they won't guess that we've lightened it for the holidays. The dressing is a creamy blend of nonfat yogurt, reduced-fat sour cream, and reduced-fat mayonnaise, sharpened with a touch of lemon juice and zest. Serve as a first course for a sit-down dinner, or in a beautiful wooden bowl as part of a buffet spread.

FAT: 5G/22%
CALORIES: 190
SATURATED FAT: 1.1G
CARBOHYDRATE: 34G
PROTEIN: 6G
CHOLESTEROL: 4MG
SODIUM: 266MG

MINIATURE CHEESE PUFFS

MAKES: 3 DOZEN
WORKING TIME: 20 MINUTES
TOTAL TIME: 50 MINUTES

*I*t's impossible to have just one of these—the peppery cheese flavor is addictive. These guiltless treats are a hit at holiday parties.

1½ cups evaporated low-fat milk

1 cup flour

⅓ cup plus 1 tablespoon grated Parmesan cheese

1¼ teaspoons baking powder

½ teaspoon salt

¼ teaspoon dry mustard

¼ teaspoon cayenne pepper

2 eggs

4 egg whites

1. In a medium saucepan, bring the evaporated milk to a boil over medium heat. Stir in the flour, ⅓ cup of the Parmesan, the baking powder, salt, mustard, and cayenne and stir vigorously until the mixture leaves the side of the pan, about 3 minutes. Transfer to a medium bowl and let cool for 5 minutes.

2. Preheat the oven to 400°. Line a large baking sheet with parchment paper.

3. One at a time, add the eggs and 3 of the egg whites to the cooled flour mixture, stirring thoroughly after each addition, until the dough is smooth and glossy. Spoon the dough into a pastry bag with no tip attached (or use a sturdy plastic bag with a bottom corner snipped off). Pipe the dough into 1-inch mounds, 1 inch apart, on the prepared baking sheet. Brush the tops with the remaining 1 egg white, sprinkle the remaining 1 tablespoon Parmesan over, and bake for 20 minutes.

4. Reduce the oven to 350° and bake for 5 minutes longer, or until the cheese puffs are lightly golden. Place on a platter and serve.

Helpful hint: The puffs can be baked 1 day ahead and kept airtight at room temperature. Reheat in a 350° oven for about 5 minutes.

VALUES ARE PER PUFF
FAT: 0.8G/22%
CALORIES: 32
SATURATED FAT: 0.2G
CARBOHYDRATE: 4G
PROTEIN: 2G
CHOLESTEROL: 14MG
SODIUM: 84MG

MAIN COURSES

2

Everyone has a recipe for the grand holiday star, roast turkey. But give our easy version a try and it may become your very own favorite. We add extra flavor by rubbing the breast meat with herbed olive oil, and the cavity with lemon. Be sure to stuff the turkey right before roasting—never in advance. For more details on stuffing, trussing, and making gravy, see page eight.

Stuffed Roast Turkey

Serves: 12
Working time: 55 minutes
Total time: 4 hours 25 minutes

1 tablespoon olive oil

1 teaspoon dried sage

1 teaspoon dried rosemary

1 teaspoon salt

¼ teaspoon freshly ground black pepper

14-pound fresh turkey (giblets reserved for giblet broth; see tip)

1 lemon, halved

Herbed Corn Bread Stuffing (p. 38), prepared through step 3 and cooled completely

1½ cups reduced-sodium chicken broth, defatted

2 cups giblet broth (see tip) or reduced-sodium chicken broth, defatted

2 tablespoons flour

1. Preheat the oven to 350°. In a small bowl, combine the oil, sage, rosemary, salt, and pepper. Carefully loosen the skin from the turkey breast, leaving the skin intact. Rub the herb mixture under the skin and into the meat. Rub the body cavity with the lemon. Loosely spoon one-third of the stuffing into the body and neck cavities. Truss the turkey. Spoon the remaining stuffing into a 9 x 9-inch baking dish, add ½ cup of the chicken broth, cover with foil, and set aside.

2. Spray a rack in a large roasting pan with nonstick cooking spray. Place the turkey, breast-side down, on the rack. Roast for 3 hours, basting every 30 minutes with some of the remaining 1 cup chicken broth. Turn the turkey breast-side up and brush with the remaining chicken broth. Place the stuffing in the oven with the turkey and roast for 30 minutes longer, or until an instant-read thermometer inserted into the thickest part of the turkey thigh without touching the bone registers 180°. Place the turkey on a platter and let stand for 15 minutes.

3. Pour off the fat from the roasting pan. Place the pan over medium heat and add the giblet broth, stirring to loosen the browned bits. Place the flour in a small saucepan, and gradually whisk in the giblet mixture over medium heat until combined. Cook, whisking, until the gravy is thickened, about 5 minutes. Serve the turkey with the gravy and stuffing. Remove the turkey skin before eating.

Fat: 16g/27%
Calories: 534
Saturated Fat: 4.5g
Carbohydrate: 14g
Protein: 80g
Cholesterol: 201mg
Sodium: 925mg

TIP

To prepare giblet broth for gravy, in a medium saucepan, combine the turkey giblets (except the liver, which would add a bitter taste) and water to cover by 2 inches. Bring to a boil, skimming off any foam. Add onion, a bay leaf, and celery and carrot chunks and simmer for about 1 hour while the turkey roasts. Add more water as needed to be sure you end up with 2 cups of broth. Strain the mixture through a sieve lined with dampened paper towels; discard the solids.

Herbed Corn Bread Stuffing

Makes: 8 cups
Working time: 20 minutes
Total time: 50 minutes

Brightly flecked with red bell peppers and parsley, and crunchy with pine nuts, this moist corn bread stuffing will appeal to everyone.

⅔ cup coarsely chopped dried apricots

¼ cup brandy

1 teaspoon olive oil

5 shallots, finely chopped

3 cloves garlic, minced

2 red bell peppers, diced

3 tablespoons pine nuts

Herbed Corn Bread (p. 80), crumbled

½ cup chopped fresh parsley

1 teaspoon dried sage

1 teaspoon dried rosemary

1 teaspoon salt

½ teaspoon freshly ground black pepper

2 cups reduced-sodium chicken broth, defatted

1. In a small bowl, combine the apricots and brandy and let stand while you prepare the vegetable mixture.

2. Meanwhile, in a large nonstick skillet, heat the oil until hot but not smoking over medium heat. Add the shallots and garlic and cook, stirring frequently, until the shallots are softened, about 5 minutes. Add the bell peppers and cook, stirring frequently, until the peppers are softened, about 5 minutes.

3. Stir in the pine nuts and transfer to a large bowl. Add the corn bread, parsley, sage, rosemary, salt, and black pepper and stir well to combine. Add the broth and the apricot mixture and stir until the corn bread is moistened.

4. Transfer to a 2½-quart baking dish, cover with foil, and bake for 30 minutes, or until the stuffing is piping hot. Spoon the stuffing into a medium bowl and serve.

Helpful hints: Homemade corn bread makes this stuffing special—for best results, make it 1 day ahead and cut it into squares so it can dry out. Or, you can substitute 8 cups of crumbled store-bought corn bread. The stuffing can be made earlier in the day and refrigerated in the baking dish. While it's fine to prepare the stuffing ahead, remember, never stuff a bird until just before you're ready to roast.

VALUES ARE PER ½ CUP
FAT: 2G/28%
CALORIES: 56
SATURATED FAT: 0.3G
CARBOHYDRATE: 9G
PROTEIN: 2G
CHOLESTEROL: 0.3MG
SODIUM: 270MG

MAKES: 11 CUPS
WORKING TIME: 30 MINUTES
TOTAL TIME: 1 HOUR 15 MINUTES

1 pound fresh chestnuts

15 ounces Italian or French bread, cut into ½-inch squares (about 10 cups)

2 teaspoons olive oil

4 ounces turkey sausage, coarsely chopped

6 shallots, finely chopped

3 ribs celery, halved lengthwise and thinly sliced

3 cups reduced-sodium chicken broth, defatted

½ cup chopped fresh parsley

1 teaspoon dried thyme

¾ teaspoon salt

½ teaspoon freshly ground black pepper

½ teaspoon dried sage

1. With a sharp paring knife, cut an "X" into the flat side of each chestnut. In a large saucepan of boiling water, cook the chestnuts until tender, 15 to 20 minutes. Drain well. When cool enough to handle, peel the chestnuts, coarsely chop, and set aside.

2. Meanwhile, preheat the oven to 350°. Spread the bread on a baking sheet and bake for 7 to 10 minutes, stirring occasionally, or until lightly golden and crisp. Transfer to a large bowl. Keep the oven on.

3. In a large nonstick skillet, heat the oil until hot but not smoking over medium heat. Add the sausage and cook until the sausage is lightly browned, about 5 minutes. Add the shallots and cook, stirring frequently, until the shallots are softened, about 5 minutes. Stir in the celery and cook until the celery is tender, about 5 minutes. Add to the bread along with the chestnuts, broth, parsley, thyme, salt, pepper, and sage and stir well to combine.

4. Transfer to a 3-quart baking dish, cover with foil, and bake for 30 minutes, or until the stuffing is piping hot. Spoon the stuffing into a large bowl and serve.

Helpful hints: Prepare the stuffing earlier in the day and refrigerate. To reheat leftovers in the microwave, place in a microwave-safe casserole, cover, and microwave on high power for 3 minutes, stirring often.

VALUES ARE PER ½ CUP
FAT: 2G/15%
CALORIES: 131
SATURATED FAT: 0.5G
CARBOHYDRATE: 24G
PROTEIN: 4G
CHOLESTEROL: 3MG
SODIUM: 321MG

Holiday time is about delicious indulgences, and this stuffing is certainly that—chestnuts add a very rich flavor.

Roast Chicken with Classic Bread Stuffing

SERVES: 4
WORKING TIME: 35 MINUTES
TOTAL TIME: 2 HOURS

This holiday classic could easily become a special family request for dinner at any time of the year. The whole chicken is aromatically flavored with lemon and herbs tucked under the skin. Serve with a bakery bread, such as braided challah, and garnish with cherry tomatoes and flat-leaf parsley. Let the chicken stand for fifteen minutes before carving so the juices can settle.

9 ounces white sandwich bread, cut into ½-inch cubes (about 6 cups)

2 teaspoons vegetable oil

1 large onion, diced

2 ribs celery, halved lengthwise and cut into thin slices

3 cloves garlic, minced

1½ cups reduced-sodium chicken broth, defatted

1 teaspoon dried tarragon

1 teaspoon dried rosemary

½ teaspoon salt

3½-pound whole chicken

2 tablespoons fresh lemon juice

1. Preheat the oven to 375°. Spread the bread on a baking sheet and bake for 7 minutes, stirring occasionally, or until lightly golden and crisp. Transfer to a large bowl. Keep the oven on. Meanwhile, in a large nonstick skillet, heat the oil until hot but not smoking over medium heat. Add the onion, celery, and garlic and cook, stirring frequently, until the vegetables are tender, about 7 minutes. Add to the bread along with 1¼ cups of the broth, ½ teaspoon of the tarragon, ½ teaspoon of the rosemary, and the salt and stir well to mix.

2. Carefully loosen the skin from the chicken breast, leaving the skin intact. Rub the lemon juice under the skin and into the meat, then rub the remaining ½ teaspoon tarragon and remaining ½ teaspoon rosemary into the meat. Loosely spoon about one-third of the stuffing into the chicken cavity. Truss the chicken by tying together the legs with string. Spoon the remaining stuffing into an 8 x 8-inch baking dish, cover with foil, and set aside.

3. Place the chicken on a rack in a small roasting pan and roast for 20 minutes. Brush with some of the remaining ¼ cup broth and continue to roast for 1¼ hours longer, basting every 15 minutes with the broth, or until the chicken is cooked through. During the last 30 minutes of roasting, place the stuffing in the oven with the chicken. Spoon the stuffing into a medium bowl and place the chicken on a platter. Remove the chicken skin before eating.

FAT: 15G/28%
CALORIES: 499
SATURATED FAT: 3.7G
CARBOHYDRATE: 39G
PROTEIN: 49G
CHOLESTEROL: 127MG
SODIUM: 1,000MG

OYSTER STUFFING

MAKES: 8 CUPS
WORKING TIME: 25 MINUTES
TOTAL TIME: 1 HOUR 5 MINUTES

14 ounces whole-wheat bread, cut into ½-inch squares (about 9 cups)

2 teaspoons olive oil

1 large onion, finely chopped

2 cloves garlic, minced

2 ribs celery, halved lengthwise and thinly sliced

1 teaspoon unsalted butter

1 to 1½ cups reduced-sodium chicken broth, defatted

1 cup shucked oysters, ½ cup liquor reserved

½ cup chopped fresh parsley

¾ teaspoon dried marjoram or oregano

¾ teaspoon dried tarragon

¼ teaspoon salt

1. Preheat the oven to 350°. Spread the bread on a baking sheet and bake for 7 to 10 minutes, stirring occasionally, or until lightly golden and crisp. Transfer to a large bowl. Keep the oven on.

2. Meanwhile, in a large nonstick skillet, heat the oil until hot but not smoking over medium heat. Add the onion and garlic and cook, stirring frequently, until the onion is softened, about 7 minutes. Add the celery and cook, stirring frequently, until the celery is tender, about 5 minutes longer.

3. Add the celery mixture to the bread along with the butter and toss until the butter is melted. Add 1 cup of the broth, the oysters, reserved ½ cup oyster liquor (if you don't have enough oyster liquor, add up to another ½ cup broth), parsley, marjoram, tarragon, and salt and toss well to combine.

4. Transfer to a 2½-quart baking dish, cover with foil, and bake for 30 minutes, or until the oysters are cooked through and the stuffing is piping hot. Spoon the stuffing into a medium bowl and serve.

Helpful hints: To ensure the best flavor, prepare the stuffing just before baking. Reheat leftovers in a low oven, covered, to avoid toughening the oysters. Add a little more broth if the stuffing seems dry.

VALUES ARE PER ½ CUP
FAT: 2G/23%
CALORIES: 88
SATURATED FAT: 0.5G
CARBOHYDRATE: 14G
PROTEIN: 4G
CHOLESTEROL: 9MG
SODIUM: 228MG

The nutty flavor of the toasted whole-wheat bread complements the brininess of the oysters in this rich stuffing. Excellent with fowl, it also partners deliciously with beef roasts. Buy oysters from a reliable source—the shells should be tightly closed and unbroken, or if slightly open, should close when tapped. Refrigerate oysters for no more than one day, over wet paper towels in an open container.

If all your holiday guests prefer white meat, our whole roasted turkey breast, with its separately baked wild and pecan rice stuffing, is the perfect culinary solution. Have your butcher cut away and remove the backbone, and then crack the breastbone so the breast will lie flat. For the traditional touch, serve with cranberry sauce.

Turkey Breast with Wild Rice Stuffing

SERVES: 8
WORKING TIME: 30 MINUTES
TOTAL TIME: 3 HOURS

4 cups reduced-sodium chicken broth, defatted

2 carrots, coarsely chopped

1 large onion, finely chopped

1½ teaspoons dried thyme

1 teaspoon salt

½ teaspoon grated lemon zest

¾ cup wild rice

¾ cup pecan rice or basmati rice

¼ cup coarsely chopped pecans

3 cloves garlic, minced

¼ cup chopped fresh parsley

3 tablespoons plus 1 teaspoon fresh lemon juice

1 tablespoon olive oil

1¾ teaspoons dried rosemary

6-pound bone-in turkey breast, backbone removed and breastbone cracked

2 teaspoons cornstarch mixed with 1 tablespoon water

1. In a large pot, combine 2 cups of the broth, 1 cup of water, the carrots, onion, 1 teaspoon of the thyme, ½ teaspoon of the salt, and the lemon zest. Bring to a boil, add all the rice, and return to a boil. Reduce to a simmer, cover, and cook until the rice is tender, about 30 minutes. Stir in the pecans and cool completely.

2. Preheat the oven to 425°. In a small bowl, combine the garlic, parsley, 3 tablespoons of the lemon juice, the oil, 1 teaspoon of the rosemary, remaining ½ teaspoon thyme, and remaining ½ teaspoon salt. Loosen the skin from the turkey breast, leaving the skin intact. Rub the mixture under the skin and into the meat. Transfer the rice mixture to an 8 x 8-inch baking dish and place the dish in a roasting pan. Pour 1 cup of the broth and 2 cups of water into the roasting pan (see tip; top photo) along with the remaining ¾ teaspoon rosemary. Place a wire rack over the stuffing, place the turkey on the rack (bottom photo), and roast for 1 hour. Reduce the oven to 350° and roast for 1 hour longer, or until the turkey is cooked through. Place the turkey on a platter. Remove the dish of stuffing.

3. Strain the pan juices into a small saucepan, skim the fat, and add the remaining 1 cup broth. Bring to a boil, stir in the cornstarch mixture and remaining 1 teaspoon lemon juice, and cook, stirring, until thickened, about 1 minute. Carve the turkey and serve with the gravy and stuffing. Remove the turkey skin before eating.

FAT: 6G/12%
CALORIES: 459
SATURATED FAT: 1G
CARBOHYDRATE: 29G
PROTEIN: 70G
CHOLESTEROL: 176MG
SODIUM: 723MG

Place the dish of stuffing in a roasting pan, then pour the broth mixture into the roasting pan around the dish. This liquid will form the basis for the gravy. Place the turkey breast on a rack set over the stuffing so it will absorb some of the juices from the turkey.

FILET STEAKS WITH NEW POTATOES AND LEEKS

SERVES: 4
WORKING TIME: 25 MINUTES
TOTAL TIME: 55 MINUTES

For some meat lovers, only a sumptuous steak will satisfy—even during the holidays, when poultry seems to be the favorite. These robustly flavored filet steaks, seasoned with rosemary and thyme, are colorfully accented with garlicky roasted vegetables for a no-fuss one-pan meal. To enhance the festive spirit, pour a good Champagne.

¾ teaspoon salt

½ teaspoon dried rosemary

½ teaspoon dried thyme

¼ teaspoon freshly ground black pepper

1 clove garlic, minced, plus 2 cloves garlic, peeled

4 filet mignon steaks (about 3½ ounces each), ½ inch thick

1½ pounds small red potatoes

2½ teaspoons olive oil

4 leeks, halved lengthwise and cut into 2-inch pieces

2 red bell peppers, cut into 1-inch squares

1. In a small bowl, combine ¼ teaspoon of the salt, the rosemary, thyme, black pepper, and minced garlic. Rub the mixture into the steaks and let stand while you prepare the vegetables.

2. Preheat the oven to 425°. With a vegetable peeler, remove a narrow strip from around the middle of each potato (this creates a nicer appearance). In a large pot of boiling water, cook the potatoes for 10 minutes (potatoes will not be tender). Drain well; pat dry.

3. In a large baking pan, combine the oil and peeled garlic and heat in the oven for 4 minutes, or until the oil is hot but not smoking. Add the potatoes, tossing to coat. Roast for 10 minutes, or until the potatoes are lightly golden. Add the leeks and bell peppers, tossing to coat. Sprinkle with the remaining ½ teaspoon salt and continue to roast for 10 minutes, or until the vegetables are almost tender.

4. Meanwhile, spray a large nonstick skillet with nonstick cooking spray, then heat until hot but not smoking over medium-high heat. Add the steaks and cook until the bottoms are lightly browned, about 2 minutes. Place the steaks, browned-side up, over the vegetables and continue to roast for 7 minutes longer, or until the steaks are medium-rare and the vegetables are tender. Divide the steaks and vegetables among 4 plates and serve.

Helpful hint: Prepare the steaks and potatoes several hours ahead through step 2; refrigerate. Bring to room temperature before proceeding.

FAT: 12G/26%
CALORIES: 407
SATURATED FAT: 3.3G
CARBOHYDRATE: 50G
PROTEIN: 26G
CHOLESTEROL: 62MG
SODIUM: 502MG

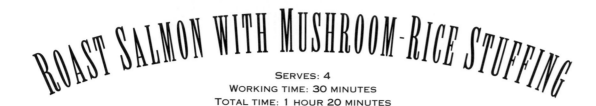

ROAST SALMON WITH MUSHROOM-RICE STUFFING

SERVES: 4
WORKING TIME: 30 MINUTES
TOTAL TIME: 1 HOUR 20 MINUTES

1 teaspoon olive oil

3 scallions, thinly sliced

1 clove garlic, minced

2 cups thinly sliced button mushrooms

2 cups thinly sliced shiitake mushrooms

⅔ cup long-grain white rice

¾ teaspoon salt

¾ teaspoon dried tarragon

¾ teaspoon dried rosemary

1¾ pounds center-cut salmon fillet

¼ cup fresh lemon juice

1 teaspoon cornstarch mixed with 1 tablespoon water

¼ cup snipped fresh dill

½ teaspoon Dijon mustard

1. In a large saucepan, heat the oil until hot but not smoking over medium heat. Add the scallions and garlic and cook, stirring frequently, until the scallions are softened, about 2 minutes. Add all the mushrooms, stirring to coat. Add ¼ cup of water and cook, stirring frequently, until the mushrooms are tender, about 7 minutes. Stir in the rice, 1½ cups of water, ½ teaspoon of the salt, ½ teaspoon of the tarragon, and ½ teaspoon of the rosemary and bring to a boil. Reduce to a simmer, cover, and cook until the rice is tender, about 20 minutes. Transfer to a small roasting pan, fluff with a fork, and let cool for about 10 minutes.

2. Preheat the oven to 425°. Lay the salmon flat, flesh-side up. Rub the remaining ¼ teaspoon salt, ¼ teaspoon tarragon, and ¼ teaspoon rosemary into the salmon. Place the salmon, skin-side up, over the rice stuffing. With a small paring knife, lightly score the salmon skin and roast for 20 to 25 minutes, or until the salmon is just opaque.

3. In a small saucepan, combine the lemon juice and 2 tablespoons of water and bring to a boil over medium heat. Stir in the cornstarch mixture and cook, stirring constantly, until the sauce is slightly thickened, about 1 minute. Remove from the heat and stir in the dill and mustard. With a paring knife, remove and discard the salmon skin, cut the salmon into 4 pieces, and divide among 4 plates. Serve the salmon with the sauce and stuffing.

FAT: 14G/29%
CALORIES: 438
SATURATED FAT: 2.2G
CARBOHYDRATE: 32G
PROTEIN: 44G
CHOLESTEROL: 109MG
SODIUM: 522MG

Looking for a lighter supper to serve during the holiday season that's still elegant enough for guests? This is it. The herb-rubbed salmon is nicely complemented by the woodsy mushroom stuffing, and is topped with a tart lemon sauce. Shiitake mushrooms are a meaty Oriental variety with an almost steak-like flavor. Choose plump, unblemished shiitakes (broken caps are a sign of age).

CURRANT-GLAZED PORK WITH SWEET POTATO PURÉE

SERVES: 8
WORKING TIME: 40 MINUTES
TOTAL TIME: 1 HOUR 30 MINUTES

*T*his spectacular pork roast dinner is a feast of sweet and tart flavors, from the Granny Smith apples puréed with sweet potatoes to the shimmering currant glaze. And it's all extravagantly sparked with fragrant herbs and spices. Roasting the pork at an initially high temperature sears the outside and locks in the tasty juices.

3 cloves garlic, minced, plus 6 cloves garlic, thinly sliced
1 tablespoon plus ⅛ teaspoon sugar
1½ teaspoons dried sage
1 teaspoon salt
¾ teaspoon freshly ground black pepper
½ teaspoon dried rosemary
1 bay leaf, crushed
1¾ pounds boneless center-cut pork loin
¼ cup red currant jelly
2 teaspoons olive oil
2½ pounds sweet potatoes, peeled and thinly sliced
2 Granny Smith apples, peeled, cored, and thinly sliced
1½ cups apple juice
½ teaspoon ground ginger
¼ teaspoon ground allspice
½ cup evaporated low-fat milk

1. Preheat the oven to 425°. In a small bowl, combine the minced garlic, ⅛ teaspoon of the sugar, ¾ teaspoon of the sage, ¼ teaspoon of the salt, ¼ teaspoon of the pepper, the rosemary, and bay leaf. Rub the mixture into the pork. Place the pork in a small baking pan and roast for 15 minutes.

2. In a small saucepan, warm the jelly over low heat until the jelly is melted. Brush the jelly over the pork. Reduce the oven to 350° and continue to roast for 30 minutes longer, brushing every 10 minutes with the jelly, or until the pork is glistening and cooked through.

3. Meanwhile, in a large nonstick skillet, heat the oil until hot but not smoking over medium heat. Add the sweet potatoes, apples, and sliced garlic, stirring to coat. Sprinkle with the remaining 1 tablespoon sugar and cook, stirring frequently, until the potatoes are barely tender, about 15 minutes.

4. Stir in the apple juice, remaining ¾ teaspoon sage, remaining ¾ teaspoon salt, remaining ½ teaspoon pepper, the ginger, and allspice and bring to a boil. Reduce to a simmer, cover, and cook, stirring occasionally, until the potatoes are tender, about 15 minutes longer. Transfer to a large bowl, add the evaporated milk, and mash the mixture until creamy but still a little lumpy. Thinly slice the pork, divide among 8 plates, and serve with the potato purée.

FAT: 9G/22%
CALORIES: 358
SATURATED FAT: 2.7G
CARBOHYDRATE: 46G
PROTEIN: 24G
CHOLESTEROL: 61MG
SODIUM: 359MG

Kasha and Bow-Tie Stuffing

MAKES: 12 CUPS
WORKING TIME: 25 MINUTES
TOTAL TIME: 1 HOUR 5 MINUTES

Our classic eastern European pairing of grain and pasta makes a delicious, nutty-scented stuffing for poultry as well as an inviting side dish.

4 ounces farfalle (bow-tie) pasta or small elbow macaroni

2 cups kasha (buckwheat groats)

1 egg, lightly beaten

2 cups reduced-sodium chicken broth, defatted

1¼ teaspoons salt

½ teaspoon dried thyme

¼ teaspoon freshly ground black pepper

2 tablespoons olive oil

6 scallions, thinly sliced

3 cloves garlic, minced

1 carrot, diced

1 red bell pepper, diced

3 cups thinly sliced mushrooms

2 teaspoons grated lemon zest

1 tablespoon fresh lemon juice

1. In a medium saucepan of boiling water, cook the pasta until just tender. Drain well and transfer to a large bowl.

2. Meanwhile, in a medium bowl, combine the kasha and egg and stir to blend. In a large dry skillet, cook the kasha mixture over medium heat, stirring constantly, until the kernels are separate and lightly toasted, about 4 minutes. Gradually stir in the broth and ½ cup of water. Add the salt, thyme, and black pepper and bring to a boil. Reduce to a simmer, cover, and cook until the kasha is tender and the liquid has been absorbed, about 15 minutes.

3. Meanwhile, preheat the oven to 350°. In a large nonstick skillet, heat 1 tablespoon of the oil until hot but not smoking over medium heat. Add the scallions and garlic and cook, stirring frequently, until the scallions are very tender and lightly browned, about 5 minutes. Stir in the carrot and bell pepper and cook until the vegetables are tender, about 5 minutes. Stir in the mushrooms and cook until the mushrooms are tender, about 5 minutes.

4. Add the vegetable mixture, kasha mixture, remaining 1 tablespoon oil, the lemon zest, and lemon juice to the pasta and toss well to combine. Transfer to a 3½-quart baking dish, cover with foil, and bake for 30 minutes, or until the stuffing is piping hot. Spoon the stuffing into a large bowl and serve.

VALUES ARE PER ½ CUP
FAT: 2G/19%
CALORIES: 86
SATURATED FAT: 0.3G
CARBOHYDRATE: 15G
PROTEIN: 3G
CHOLESTEROL: 9MG
SODIUM: 174MG

ORANGE-GLAZED CARROTS

MAKES: 4 CUPS
WORKING TIME: 20 MINUTES
TOTAL TIME: 40 MINUTES

2 pounds carrots, cut lengthwise into thirds, then into 2-inch pieces

¾ teaspoon finely julienned orange zest

1½ cups fresh orange juice

2 cloves garlic, minced

⅓ cup thinly sliced scallion whites

1 tablespoon firmly packed light brown sugar

2 teaspoons unsalted butter

1 teaspoon ground ginger

½ teaspoon salt

¼ cup thinly sliced scallion greens

1. In a large saucepan, combine the carrots, orange zest, orange juice, garlic, scallion whites, brown sugar, butter, ginger, and salt. Bring to a boil over medium heat and cook gently, stirring occasionally, until the carrots are tender and glossy and the liquid is syrupy, about 20 minutes.

2. Stir in the scallion greens until well combined. Spoon the carrots into a medium bowl and serve.

Helpful hints: Plan on buying 5 or 6 oranges for the needed amount of juice. This can be prepared up to 1 day ahead through step 1. To serve, gently reheat, stirring occasionally, on the stovetop over low heat or in a microwave on half power. Mix in the scallion greens just before serving.

VALUES ARE PER ½ CUP
FAT: 1G/13%
CALORIES: 88
SATURATED FAT: 0.6G
CARBOHYDRATE: 19G
PROTEIN: 2G
CHOLESTEROL: 3MG
SODIUM: 179MG

For this simple and appealing side dish, the tartness of orange deliciously underscores the sweetness of carrots. And we've added a subtle Oriental touch by enlivening the taste with a little ginger. These carrots look especially inviting on a big buffet table with other great holiday staples—orange yams, green beans, ruby red cranberry sauce, and a golden bird.

These
heavenly biscuits are
slightly crusty on the
outside and pleasingly
airy on the inside,
thanks to the leavening
action of both the yeast
and baking powder,
plus the technique of
folding the dough into
layers. A basket of
these will disappear
quickly, since they pair
well with any dish,
from a glazed loin of
pork to a stuffed roast
chicken.

Angel Biscuits

Makes: 12 biscuits
Working time: 15 minutes
Total time: 50 minutes (includes rising time)

¾ teaspoon active dry yeast
1 tablespoon sugar
2 cups flour
3 teaspoons baking powder
½ teaspoon baking soda
½ teaspoon salt
2 tablespoons unsalted butter
¾ cup low-fat (1.5%) buttermilk

1. Place ¼ cup of warm water in a small bowl. Sprinkle the yeast and ½ teaspoon of the sugar on top and let stand until the mixture is foamy, about 5 minutes.

2. Meanwhile, in a large bowl, combine the flour, the remaining 2½ teaspoons of sugar, the baking powder, baking soda, and salt and stir well to blend. With a pastry blender or 2 knives, cut in the butter until the mixture resembles coarse meal.

3. Add the buttermilk to the yeast mixture and stir to blend. Make a well in the center of the flour mixture, pour in the buttermilk mixture, and stir until just combined. Cover with plastic wrap and set aside in a warm place for 20 minutes (the biscuits will not double).

4. Preheat the oven to 425°. On a lightly floured board, roll the dough into a large rectangle. Fold the dough over onto itself, making 4 layers (see tip), then roll into a 10 x 5-inch rectangle about ½ inch thick. With a 2-inch biscuit cutter, cut out biscuits. Gather the scraps, reroll about ½ inch thick, and cut out more biscuits. Place the biscuits, 2 inches apart, on a nonstick baking sheet and bake for 15 minutes, or until the biscuits are lightly golden.

Helpful hint: Although the biscuits are best served straight from the oven, they can be baked 1 day ahead and held at room temperature in an airtight container. Gently rewarm in a low oven.

VALUES ARE PER BISCUIT
Fat: 2g/19%
Calories: 110
Saturated Fat: 1.4g
Carbohydrate: 19g
Protein: 3g
Cholesterol: 6mg
Sodium: 274mg

TIP

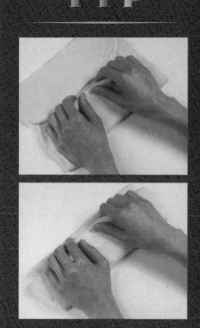

To prepare the biscuits, fold the 2 short sides of the rolled-out dough over so they meet in the middle. Then fold one half over on top of the other half, creating 4 layers that will puff during baking.

BOURBON-GLAZED YAMS

MAKES: 4 CUPS
WORKING TIME: 20 MINUTES
TOTAL TIME: 1 HOUR 10 MINUTES

You can't beat the homey goodness of these yams, made sweet, tart, and mellow with brown sugar, pineapple juice, and bourbon.

2 pounds yams or sweet potatoes
2 teaspoons unsalted butter
3 tablespoons firmly packed light brown sugar
¼ cup pineapple juice
1 tablespoon fresh lime juice
½ teaspoon salt
⅛ teaspoon ground allspice
⅛ teaspoon ground nutmeg
3 tablespoons bourbon
¼ cup minced scallions

1. Preheat the oven to 450°. With a fork, prick the yams in several places. Place on a baking sheet and bake for 45 minutes, or until the yams are tender. When cool enough to handle, peel the yams and cut crosswise into 1½-inch slices.

2. In a large skillet, melt the butter over medium heat. Add the brown sugar and stir to blend. Add the pineapple juice, lime juice, salt, allspice, and nutmeg and cook until the mixture is bubbly, about 2 minutes. Stir in the yams and cook, gently turning occasionally, until the yams are glazed and nicely coated, about 10 minutes.

3. Remove the pan from the heat and add the bourbon. Bring the mixture to a boil over high heat and cook until the bourbon has evaporated, about 2 minutes. Stir in the scallions. Spoon the yams into a medium bowl and serve.

Helpful hints: The yams can be prepared 1 day ahead through step 1, then refrigerated. Bring to room temperature before proceeding. Leftovers can be made into a delightful winter soup: Purée the yams in a food processor with a little chicken broth, and then gently reheat, stirring in more broth or skim milk to reach the desired consistency.

VALUES ARE PER ½ CUP
FAT: 1G/6%
CALORIES: 162
SATURATED FAT: 0.6G
CARBOHYDRATE: 34G
PROTEIN: 2G
CHOLESTEROL: 3MG
SODIUM: 158MG

CRANBERRY-POACHED HERBED APPLES

MAKES: 2½ CUPS
WORKING TIME: 15 MINUTES
TOTAL TIME: 30 MINUTES

6-ounce can frozen cranberry juice concentrate, thawed

¼ cup red currant jelly

2 bay leaves

½ teaspoon dried sage

½ teaspoon dried rosemary

½ teaspoon salt

½ teaspoon freshly ground black pepper

4 large Granny Smith or Empire apples, peeled, cored, and cut into 2-inch chunks

1. In a large saucepan, stir together the juice concentrate, jelly, bay leaves, sage, rosemary, salt, and pepper. Bring to a boil over medium heat, add the apples, and reduce to a very gentle boil. Cook, stirring frequently, until the apples are tender, about 10 minutes. With a slotted spoon, transfer the apples to a medium serving bowl and set aside.

2. Increase the heat to high and cook the juice mixture until it is reduced to a light syrup, about 5 minutes.

3. Strain the sauce, discarding the solids. Spoon the sauce over the apples and serve.

Helpful hints: This can also be chilled and served cold to accompany a platter of leftover sliced turkey or other meats. For a more relish-like appearance, cut the apple into small dice, and then reduce the initial cooking time slightly.

VALUES ARE PER ½ CUP
FAT: 1G/0.2%
CALORIES: 197
SATURATED FAT: 0.1G
CARBOHYDRATE: 51G
PROTEIN: 0G
CHOLESTEROL: 0MG
SODIUM: 227MG

This savory, chutney-like side dish is the perfect accompaniment to rich holiday meats, such as turkey and pork.

BROWN AND WILD RICE PILAF

MAKES: 6 CUPS
WORKING TIME: 30 MINUTES
TOTAL TIME: 1 HOUR 5 MINUTES

½ cup wild rice

2 teaspoons olive oil

1 large onion, coarsely chopped

3 cloves garlic, minced

2 cups thickly sliced mushrooms

1 carrot, thinly sliced

1 green bell pepper, diced

2 cups reduced-sodium chicken broth, defatted

1 cup long-grain brown rice

½ teaspoon dried rosemary

½ teaspoon dried sage

¼ teaspoon salt

¼ teaspoon freshly ground black pepper

1. In a small bowl, combine the wild rice with cold water to cover. Let stand while you cook the vegetable mixture.

2. In a large saucepan, heat the oil until hot but not smoking over medium heat. Add the onion and garlic and cook, stirring frequently, until the onion is tender, about 7 minutes. Stir in the mushrooms, carrot, and bell pepper and cook, stirring frequently, until the vegetables are tender, about 5 minutes.

3. Drain the wild rice and add to the pan, stirring to coat. Stir in the broth, brown rice, 2 cups of water, the rosemary, sage, salt, and black pepper. Bring to a boil, reduce to a simmer, cover, and cook until the rice is tender, about 35 minutes.

Helpful hints: You may use all brown rice for this dish. Also, feel free to experiment with exotic fresh mushrooms, such as shiitake, portobello, or chanterelle. The pilaf can be prepared several hours ahead. To serve, gently reheat in the top of a steamer.

VALUES ARE PER ½ CUP
FAT: 1G/12%
CALORIES: 106
SATURATED FAT: 0.2G
CARBOHYDRATE: 21G
PROTEIN: 3G
CHOLESTEROL: 0MG
SODIUM: 157MG

Wild rice is actually the seed of a marsh grass native to the Great Lakes region, and not a rice at all. It tastes delicious in this nutty-sweet dish, which gets its woodsy flavor from mushrooms, rosemary, and sage. If you have attractive cookware, place the saucepan, with a trivet, directly on the holiday table. This pilaf is ideal alongside roast poultry, or inside as a stuffing.

SHALLOT-TOPPED GARLIC MASHED POTATOES

MAKES: 8 CUPS
WORKING TIME: 30 MINUTES
TOTAL TIME: 50 MINUTES

What sets these sensational mashed potatoes apart is both the garlic and the caramelized shallots, which add a deep, rich flavor.

4 teaspoons olive oil

1¼ pounds shallots, thinly sliced (about 4 cups)

2 teaspoons sugar

1 cup reduced-sodium chicken broth, defatted

1¼ teaspoons salt

3½ pounds baking potatoes, peeled and cut into large chunks

16 cloves garlic, peeled

¼ teaspoon ground nutmeg

2 bay leaves

1 cup evaporated low-fat milk

1. In a large nonstick skillet, heat 2 teaspoons of the oil until hot but not smoking over medium heat. Add the shallots, sprinkle with the sugar, and cook, stirring frequently, until the shallots are glazed, 5 to 8 minutes. Add the broth and ¼ teaspoon of the salt and cook, stirring occasionally, until the shallots are tender and golden brown, about 7 minutes longer. Set aside; cover with foil.

2. Meanwhile, in a large pot, combine the potatoes, garlic, nutmeg, bay leaves and enough cold water to cover. Bring to a boil and add ½ teaspoon of the salt. Reduce to a simmer and cook until the potatoes are tender, about 20 minutes. Drain well. Discard the bay leaves.

3. Transfer the potatoes and garlic to a large bowl and mash until the mixture is smooth. Add the evaporated milk, remaining 2 teaspoons oil, and remaining ½ teaspoon of salt and mash until the mixture is thick and creamy. Spoon the mashed potatoes into a medium serving bowl, spoon the shallot mixture on top, and serve.

Helpful hints: You can replace the shallots with 4 large onions, thinly sliced. If you have leftover mashed potatoes, stir in enough chicken broth and/or skim milk to thin for a potato soup. Or, for a brunch dish, stir an egg white into the potatoes, shape into patties, and sauté in a nonstick skillet coated with nonstick cooking spray.

VALUES ARE PER ½ CUP
FAT: 2G/12%
CALORIES: 115
SATURATED FAT: 0.2G
CARBOHYDRATE: 22G
PROTEIN: 4G
CHOLESTEROL: 3MG
SODIUM: 237MG

CREAMED ONIONS

MAKES: 4 CUPS
WORKING TIME: 20 MINUTES
TOTAL TIME: 55 MINUTES

1½ pounds small white onions, peeled

1 teaspoon unsalted butter

1 teaspoon sugar

2 tablespoons flour

2¼ cups low-fat (1%) milk

¾ teaspoon salt

½ teaspoon dried thyme

¼ teaspoon freshly ground black pepper

¼ cup finely chopped fresh parsley

1. In a large pot of boiling water, cook the onions for 2 minutes to blanch. Drain well.

2. In a large nonstick skillet, melt the butter over low heat. Add the onions, sprinkle the sugar over, and cook, shaking the pan frequently, until the onions are lightly golden and glazed, about 5 minutes.

3. Meanwhile, place the flour in a medium saucepan, and gradually whisk in the milk over medium heat until no lumps remain. Bring to a boil and whisk in the salt, thyme, and pepper. Reduce to a simmer and cook, whisking frequently, until the sauce is slightly thickened, about 5 minutes.

4. Pour the sauce over the onions, add the parsley, and stir well to combine. Return the pan to low heat, cover, and cook until the onions are tender, about 25 minutes. Spoon the creamed onions into a medium bowl and serve.

Helpful hint: The onions and white sauce can be prepared earlier in the day and stored separately in the refrigerator. To serve, proceed with step 4 of the recipe.

VALUES ARE PER ½ CUP
FAT: 1G/15%
CALORIES: 76
SATURATED FAT: 0.7G
CARBOHYDRATE: 13G
PROTEIN: 4G
CHOLESTEROL: 4MG
SODIUM: 250MG

*N*o *holiday buffet would be complete without this all-time favorite— made with a low-fat white sauce, not cream.*

Corn Pudding

MAKES: 5 CUPS
WORKING TIME: 10 MINUTES
TOTAL TIME: 1 HOUR 5 MINUTES

Often the tried-and-true holiday classics remain the best—as is the case with scrumptious corn pudding. Here we've reduced the fat, but have kept in the custardy goodness. This dish works very well for a buffet, since it stays flavorful even at room temperature.

3 tablespoons flour
2 cups low-fat (1%) milk
2 whole eggs
1 egg white
1 tablespoon sugar
¾ teaspoon salt
½ teaspoon dried thyme
½ teaspoon freshly ground black pepper
5 cups frozen corn kernels, thawed and well drained
1 teaspoon chopped fresh parsley

1. Preheat the oven to 325°. Spray a shallow 1½-quart baking dish with nonstick cooking spray.

2. Place the flour in a large saucepan, and gradually whisk in the milk over medium heat until no lumps remain. Bring to a boil, reduce to a simmer and cook, whisking frequently, until the mixture is very slightly thickened, about 2 minutes. Remove from the heat. In a medium bowl, whisk together the whole eggs, egg white, sugar, salt, thyme, and pepper. Gradually whisk about ½ cup of the hot milk mixture into the egg mixture, whisking constantly.

3. Whisk the warmed egg mixture back into the saucepan and cook, whisking constantly, just until the mixture is thick enough to coat the back of a spoon, about 3 minutes. Stir in the corn.

4. Spoon the mixture into the prepared baking dish and place the baking dish in a large roasting pan. Add enough hot water to the roasting pan to come halfway up the sides of the baking dish and bake for 50 to 55 minutes, or until the pudding is just set. Remove the corn pudding from the water, sprinkle the parsley on top, and serve.

Helpful hints: You can prepare the corn pudding 2 hours ahead and hold it at room temperature. Canned corn kernels can be substituted for the frozen. Be sure to drain the corn well to avoid a watery pudding.

VALUES ARE PER ½ CUP
FAT: 2G/16%
CALORIES: 124
SATURATED FAT: 0.7G
CARBOHYDRATE: 23G
PROTEIN: 6G
CHOLESTEROL: 44MG
SODIUM: 210MG

GREEN BEANS AND TOASTED ALMONDS

MAKES: 4 CUPS
WORKING TIME: 25 MINUTES
TOTAL TIME: 35 MINUTES

2 tablespoons blanched slivered almonds

1 pound green beans, trimmed

1 teaspoon olive oil

2 large red onions, halved and thinly sliced

2 cloves garlic, slivered

1 tablespoon balsamic vinegar

½ teaspoon dried rosemary

½ teaspoon salt

1 tablespoon flour

¾ cup reduced-sodium chicken broth, defatted

1. Preheat the oven to 350°. Spread the almonds on a sheet of foil and bake, stirring occasionally, for 10 minutes, or until lightly golden and fragrant. Coarsely chop the almonds and set aside.

2. Meanwhile, in a large pot of boiling water, cook the green beans until the beans are crisp-tender, about 4 minutes (timing will vary depending upon the age of the beans). Drain, rinse under cold water, and drain again. Set aside.

3. In a large nonstick skillet, heat the oil until hot but not smoking over medium heat. Add the onions and garlic and cook, stirring frequently, until the onions are lightly browned, about 10 minutes. Stir in the vinegar, rosemary, and salt and cook until the onions are very tender, about 5 minutes longer.

4. Stir in the flour until well combined. Add the broth and bring to a boil. Reduce to a simmer and cook until the mixture is slightly thickened, about 2 minutes. Stir in the beans and cook until the beans are heated through, about 3 minutes longer. Spoon the beans into a medium dish, sprinkle the almonds on top, and serve.

Helpful hints: If balsamic vinegar is not handy, you can substitute red wine vinegar. The dish can be prepared a few hours ahead, omitting the almond garnish. Gently reheat, stirring occasionally, on the stovetop over low heat, or in the microwave on half power, then garnish.

VALUES ARE PER ½ CUP
FAT: 2G/26%
CALORIES: 63
SATURATED FAT: 0.2G
CARBOHYDRATE: 10G
PROTEIN: 3G
CHOLESTEROL: 0MG
SODIUM: 207MG

A touch of richly flavored balsamic vinegar is what makes these green beans special, along with the slow-cooked red onions. This lightly textured but assertively seasoned side dish will hold its own with such substantial entrées as a filet of beef. Bring out your best white china platter to highlight the color of this dish.

CREAMED SPINACH WITH RED BELL PEPPER

MAKES: 4 CUPS
WORKING TIME: 10 MINUTES
TOTAL TIME: 15 MINUTES

Delectably rich and visually appealing with the colors of the season, this country favorite is nice with roasted beef, pork, or poultry.

3 tablespoons flour

2¾ cups low-fat (1%) milk

1 red bell pepper, diced

2 cloves garlic, minced

¾ teaspoon dried oregano

¾ teaspoon salt

⅛ teaspoon cayenne pepper

Three 10-ounce packages frozen chopped spinach, thawed and squeezed dry

3 tablespoons coarsely grated fresh Parmesan cheese

1. Place the flour in a large saucepan, and gradually whisk in the milk over medium heat until no lumps remain. Bring to a boil, reduce to a simmer, and stir in the bell pepper, garlic, oregano, salt, and cayenne. Cook, stirring frequently, until the mixture is slightly thickened, about 5 minutes.

2. Add the spinach, stir well to coat, and cook just until the spinach is heated through, about 3 minutes longer. Spoon the creamed spinach into a medium bowl, sprinkle the Parmesan on top, and serve.

Helpful hints: Prepare the creamed spinach earlier in the day, if desired, but don't add the Parmesan until just before serving. Gently reheat, stirring frequently, over low heat. For a tasty, unique vegetable dip, process any leftovers in a blender or food processor, adding a little chicken broth or evaporated skimmed milk as needed to thin the mixture slightly.

VALUES ARE PER ½ CUP
FAT: 2G/20%
CALORIES: 87
SATURATED FAT: 1G
CARBOHYDRATE: 12G
PROTEIN: 7G
CHOLESTEROL: 5MG
SODIUM: 370MG

SPOONBREAD

SERVES: 12
WORKING TIME: 10 MINUTES
TOTAL TIME: 35 MINUTES

2½ cups low-fat (1%) milk
1 tablespoon unsalted butter
1¼ cups yellow cornmeal
1 teaspoon salt
1 teaspoon sugar
¾ teaspoon baking powder
2 eggs, lightly beaten
½ cup diced jarred roasted red pepper
¼ cup finely chopped scallions

1. Preheat the oven to 375°. Spray a 1½-quart baking pan with nonstick cooking spray. In a large saucepan, combine the milk, ⅔ cup of water, and the butter. Heat over medium-low heat just until small bubbles appear around the edges of the pan. Remove from the heat.

2. In a medium bowl, stir together the cornmeal, salt, sugar, and baking powder. Add the scalded milk mixture and stir well to combine. Quickly stir in the eggs. Fold in the roasted pepper and scallions.

3. Spoon the batter into the prepared pan and bake for 25 minutes, or until the spoonbread is just set but still creamy. Serve from the pan.

Helpful hints: Spoonbread waits for no one, so carefully time its emergence from the oven and serve piping hot. If you'd prefer a little heat, sneak in a can of chopped mild green chilies for a nontraditional holiday touch.

FAT: 3G/24%
CALORIES: 100
SATURATED FAT: 1.2G
CARBOHYDRATE: 15G
PROTEIN: 4G
CHOLESTEROL: 40MG
SODIUM: 263MG

*N*ot quite a pudding and not quite a soufflé, this creamy Southern dish is best negotiated with a spoon.

MINTED PEAS AND PEARL ONIONS

MAKES: 5 CUPS
WORKING TIME: 25 MINUTES
TOTAL TIME: 40 MINUTES

This classic will surely bring back memories—and it's still an enticing way to get everyone to eat their peas. Serve in an elegant tureen on your holiday table, and let the revelers help themselves. This is one of those side dishes that goes with practically anything.

1 teaspoon olive oil
½ pound pearl onions, peeled
2 teaspoons sugar
2 tablespoons cider vinegar
2 cloves garlic, minced
1½ cups minced scallions
Two 10-ounce packages frozen peas
3 tablespoons chopped fresh mint
½ teaspoon salt
1 teaspoon unsalted butter

1. In a large nonstick skillet, heat the oil until hot but not smoking over medium heat. Add the onions, sprinkle the sugar over, and cook, shaking the pan frequently, until the onions are lightly golden, about 2 minutes. Add the vinegar and ⅔ cup of water and bring to a boil. Reduce to a simmer, cover, and cook until the onions are tender, about 15 minutes.

2. Stir in the garlic and scallions and cook, uncovered, until the scallions are just wilted, about 2 minutes. Stir in the peas, mint, and salt and cook just until the peas are heated through, about 3 minutes. Stir in the butter and toss until the butter has melted, about 30 seconds longer. Spoon the peas and onions into a medium bowl and serve.

Helpful hints: While fresh onions are best, in a pinch you could substitute 2 cups of thawed frozen pearl onions. If good-quality fresh mint is not available, use 1 teaspoon of dried mint. This recipe can be made earlier in the day through step 1. Just before serving, proceed with step 2.

VALUES ARE PER ½ CUP
FAT: 1G/13%
CALORIES: 74
SATURATED FAT: 0.3G
CARBOHYDRATE: 13G
PROTEIN: 4G
CHOLESTEROL: 1MG
SODIUM: 179MG

Holiday Peppers

MAKES: 4 CUPS
WORKING TIME: 25 MINUTES
TOTAL TIME: 25 MINUTES

1 teaspoon olive oil

*3 red bell peppers, cut into
1½-inch squares*

*2 green bell peppers, cut into
1½-inch squares*

3 cloves garlic, minced

½ teaspoon grated orange zest

⅓ cup orange juice

*1 tablespoon no-salt-added
tomato paste*

½ teaspoon salt

½ teaspoon dried oregano

*¼ teaspoon freshly ground black
pepper*

1. In a large nonstick skillet, heat the oil until hot but not smoking over medium heat. Add the bell peppers and cook, stirring frequently, until the peppers are almost tender, about 5 minutes.

2. Stir in the garlic and cook until the garlic is fragrant, about 1 minute. Add the orange zest, orange juice, tomato paste, salt, oregano, and black pepper and cook, stirring frequently, until the peppers are tender and glossy, about 3 minutes longer. Spoon the peppers into a medium bowl and serve.

Helpful hint: Finely chop any leftovers and stir into egg-white scrambled eggs for a quick and easy brunch dish.

What could be more holiday-spirited than these red and green peppers, brightly seasoned with orange? Garnish with long, thin strips of orange zest and a light sprinkling of finely ground toasted walnuts, if desired. This robust dish would deliciously enhance a roasted beef filet or loin of pork.

VALUES ARE PER ½ CUP
FAT: 1G/21%
CALORIES: 30
SATURATED FAT: 0.1G
CARBOHYDRATE: 6G
PROTEIN: 1G
CHOLESTEROL: 0MG
SODIUM: 140MG

CAULIFLOWER WITH CHEDDAR SAUCE

MAKES: 4 CUPS
WORKING TIME: 25 MINUTES
TOTAL TIME: 30 MINUTES

Our version of this vegetable classic tastes as good as the original, even though we've cut way back on the fat. Adding vinegar to the cauliflower cooking water lends a subtle flavor to the vegetable, and also helps to keep it white. For a simple embellishment, garnish with chopped fresh parsley or chives just before serving.

3 tablespoons flour
1½ cups low-fat (1%) milk
1 cup diced onion
1 teaspoon Dijon mustard
½ teaspoon salt
¼ teaspoon cayenne pepper
1 cup finely diced red bell pepper
¼ cup plus 2 tablespoons shredded Cheddar cheese
1 tablespoon distilled white vinegar or cider vinegar
1 head cauliflower, cut into florets

1. Place the flour in a large saucepan, and gradually whisk in the milk over medium heat until no lumps remain. Bring to a boil and stir in the onion, mustard, salt, and cayenne. Reduce to a simmer and cook, stirring frequently, until the sauce is slightly thickened, about 5 minutes.

2. Stir in the bell pepper and Cheddar and cook just until the cheese has melted, about 1 minute longer. Remove from the heat.

3. Meanwhile, bring a large pot of water to a boil, add the vinegar and cauliflower, and cook until the cauliflower is tender, about 5 minutes. Drain well and transfer to a medium serving bowl. Spoon the hot sauce over the cauliflower and serve.

Helpful hint: The sauce can be made earlier in the day and refrigerated. Gently reheat in a double boiler while you cook the cauliflower.

VALUES ARE PER ½ CUP
FAT: 2G/27%
CALORIES: 81
SATURATED FAT: 1.4G
CARBOHYDRATE: 11G
PROTEIN: 5G
CHOLESTEROL: 7MG
SODIUM: 220MG

BRUSSELS SPROUTS WITH CHESTNUTS

MAKES: 4 CUPS
WORKING TIME: 25 MINUTES
TOTAL TIME: 55 MINUTES

This deeply flavored dish features fresh chestnuts, which are plentiful at holiday time. (You can freeze extra chestnuts for several months.)

1 pound fresh chestnuts

1 pound Brussels sprouts, stem ends trimmed

1 teaspoon olive oil

1 ounce Canadian bacon, slivered

1 small onion, minced

1 cup reduced-sodium chicken broth, defatted

½ teaspoon dried rosemary

½ teaspoon salt

¼ teaspoon freshly ground black pepper

1 teaspoon cornstarch mixed with 1 tablespoon water

1 teaspoon unsalted butter

1. With a sharp paring knife, cut an "X" into the flat side of each chestnut. In a large saucepan of boiling water, cook the chestnuts until tender, 15 to 20 minutes. Drain well. When cool enough to handle, peel the chestnuts and set aside.

2. Meanwhile, in another large saucepan of boiling water, cook the Brussels sprouts until the sprouts are almost tender, about 8 minutes. Drain well and set aside.

3. In a large skillet, heat the oil until hot but not smoking over low heat. Add the bacon and cook until the bacon is lightly crisped, about 5 minutes. Add the onion and cook, stirring frequently, until the onion is softened, about 5 minutes. Stir in the chestnuts, sprouts, broth, rosemary, salt, and pepper. Increase the heat to high and bring to a boil. Reduce to a simmer, cover, and cook until the sprouts are tender, about 5 minutes.

4. Stir in the cornstarch mixture and return to a boil over medium heat. Cook, stirring constantly, until the mixture is slightly thickened, about 1 minute. Stir in the butter until melted. Spoon the sprouts and chestnuts into a medium bowl and serve.

Helpful hints: Frozen Brussels sprouts and dried chestnuts can replace the fresh. Cook the dried chestnuts for 30 minutes in step 1.

VALUES ARE PER ½ CUP
FAT: 3G/14%
CALORIES: 213
SATURATED FAT: 0.8G
CARBOHYDRATE: 42G
PROTEIN: 5G
CHOLESTEROL: 3MG
SODIUM: 297MG

CREAMY MASHED RUTABAGA

Makes: 5 cups
Working time: 20 minutes
Total time: 45 minutes

1¾ pounds rutabaga, peeled and thickly sliced

1 Granny Smith apple, peeled, cored, and thickly sliced

3 cloves garlic, slivered

¾ teaspoon dried marjoram or oregano

½ teaspoon salt

3 tablespoons evaporated low-fat milk

2 tablespoons grated Parmesan cheese

2 teaspoons unsalted butter

1. In a large saucepan, combine the rutabaga, apple, garlic, marjoram, and ¼ teaspoon of the salt. Add cold water to cover by 1 inch and bring to a boil. Reduce to a simmer, cover, and cook until the rutabaga is tender, about 25 minutes. Drain well and transfer the mixture to a large bowl.

2. Add the evaporated milk, Parmesan, butter, and remaining ¼ teaspoon salt and mash until the mixture is well blended but still chunky. Spoon the rutabaga mixture onto a platter and serve.

Helpful hints: This recipe can be prepared 1 day ahead through step 1 and refrigerated. To serve, gently reheat over low heat, stirring in the remaining ingredients. If you'd prefer a smooth vegetable purée, mash the mixture with a potato masher or an electric beater until no lumps remain.

VALUES ARE PER ½ CUP
Fat: 1g/24%
Calories: 48
Saturated Fat: 0.7g
Carbohydrate: 8g
Protein: 2g
Cholesterol: 4mg
Sodium: 147mg

The apple adds a tangy sweetness to the already subtly sweet rutabaga. This is a natural with roast turkey or chicken.

Rich with the flavor of potato and sour cream, and slightly sweet from a bit of brown sugar, these old-fashioned icebox rolls are a welcome addition to any holiday table. Serve in a cloth-lined wicker basket to keep them invitingly warm. Be sure to let the dough rise for the full amount of time—the long, slow refrigerator rising gives the rolls a better flavor.

POTATO ICEBOX ROLLS

MAKES: 18 ROLLS
WORKING TIME: 20 MINUTES
TOTAL TIME: 4 HOURS 15 MINUTES (INCLUDES CHILLING TIME)

1 baking potato, peeled and diced

2 tablespoons unsalted butter

¼-ounce package active dry yeast

2 tablespoons firmly packed light brown sugar

3¾ cups flour

1½ teaspoons salt

1 egg, lightly beaten

2 tablespoons reduced-fat sour cream

3 tablespoons low-fat (1%) milk

1. In a medium saucepan of boiling water, cook the potato until tender, about 15 minutes. Drain well, reserving ¾ cup of the cooking water. Transfer the potato to a small bowl, add the butter, and mash until smooth. Meanwhile, place ¼ cup of warm water in another small bowl. Sprinkle the yeast and 1 teaspoon of the brown sugar on top and let stand until the mixture is foamy, about 5 minutes.

2. In a large bowl, combine the flour, salt, and remaining 1 tablespoon plus 2 teaspoons brown sugar. Stir in the egg, yeast mixture, mashed potato, reserved ¾ cup cooking water, and sour cream until well combined. On a lightly floured board, knead the dough until smooth and elastic, about 5 minutes. Spray a large bowl with nonstick cooking spray, add the dough, turning to coat, and cover with plastic wrap. Refrigerate for at least 3 hours or overnight.

3. Spray two 9-inch round pans with nonstick cooking spray. Punch the dough down, divide in half, and roll each half into a 10-inch circle about ½ inch thick. With a 2-inch biscuit cutter, cut out rounds (see tip; top photo). Arrange the rounds in the prepared pans (bottom photo), brush with the milk, cover, and let rise in a warm place until the rolls are almost doubled, about 20 minutes.

4. Preheat the oven to 400°. Bake for 15 minutes, or until golden.

Helpful hint: You can freeze 1 pan of rolls, unbaked, for up to 1 month.

VALUES ARE PER ROLL
FAT: 2G/15%
CALORIES: 131
SATURATED FAT: 1G
CARBOHYDRATE: 24G
PROTEIN: 4G
CHOLESTEROL: 16MG
SODIUM: 203MG

Herbed Corn Bread

MAKES: 16 SQUARES
WORKING TIME: 15 MINUTES
TOTAL TIME: 35 MINUTES

1¼ cups flour

¾ cup yellow cornmeal

1 tablespoon sugar

2½ teaspoons baking powder

½ teaspoon baking soda

½ teaspoon salt

½ teaspoon dried rosemary

½ teaspoon dried thyme

⅛ teaspoon cayenne pepper

1⅓ cups low-fat (1.5%) buttermilk

½ cup grated onion

2 tablespoons extra-virgin olive oil

2 egg whites

1. Preheat the oven to 400°. Spray an 8-inch square pan with non-stick cooking spray.

2. In a large bowl, stir together the flour, cornmeal, sugar, baking powder, baking soda, salt, rosemary, thyme, and cayenne pepper. In a small bowl, stir together the buttermilk, onion, oil, and egg whites. Make a well in the center of the cornmeal mixture, pour in the buttermilk mixture, and stir until just moistened.

3. Spoon the batter into the prepared pan and bake for 20 minutes, or until the corn bread is lightly golden. Transfer to a wire rack to cool slightly. Cut the corn bread into squares and serve.

Helpful hint: For a change, use this batter to make cornsticks. Spray a cornstick pan with nonstick cooking spray, and bake in 2 batches (most pans hold only 6 or 7 sticks) for 17 minutes per batch, yielding about 14 cornsticks. Be sure to spray the pan with more nonstick cooking spray between each batch.

VALUES ARE PER SQUARE
FAT: 2G/23%
CALORIES: 92
SATURATED FAT: 0.5G
CARBOHYDRATE: 15G
PROTEIN: 3G
CHOLESTEROL: 1MG
SODIUM: 202MG

Tangy with buttermilk and satisfyingly rich with a drizzle of olive oil, our corn bread is made even lighter with the addition of egg whites. And the rosemary, thyme, and cayenne add to the full flavor. This is excellent served with your favorite holiday poultry recipe, or crumbled and used for stuffing. Make corn bread a day or two ahead if using it for stuffing—the drier texture is desirable.

ROASTED WINTER VEGETABLES

MAKES: 4 CUPS
WORKING TIME: 20 MINUTES
TOTAL TIME: 50 MINUTES

1 pound turnips, peeled, halved, and cut into ½-inch-thick wedges

1 pound parsnips, peeled and cut into ½-inch-thick slices

¾ pound carrots, cut into ½-inch-thick slices

1 tablespoon plus 1 teaspoon olive oil

3 cloves garlic, peeled

½ teaspoon salt

¼ teaspoon freshly ground black pepper

⅛ teaspoon nutmeg

1. Preheat the oven to 400°. In a large pot of boiling water, cook the turnips, parsnips, and carrots for 5 minutes to blanch. Drain well and blot dry with paper towels.

2. In a 13 x 9-inch baking dish, combine the oil and garlic and heat in the oven for 4 minutes, or until the oil is hot but not smoking. Add the turnips, parsnips, and carrots, stirring to coat. Sprinkle with the salt, pepper, and nutmeg and bake for 20 minutes, stirring occasionally, or until the vegetables are lightly browned and tender. Spoon the vegetables into a medium bowl and serve.

Helpful hints: Feel free to vary the proportion of vegetables to suit your own taste. If there are any leftovers, mash them thoroughly with a potato masher, thin with chicken broth or skim milk or both, and gently heat in a saucepan for a warming winter soup.

R *oasting brings out the natural sweetness of these root vegetables. Garnish the dish with fresh herbs and serve with the holiday bird. When shopping, select turnips and parsnips that are small or medium size, indicating younger, sweeter vegetables. These root vegetables are at their flavorful peak during the early winter months.*

VALUES ARE PER ½ CUP
FAT: 3G/26%
CALORIES: 87
SATURATED FAT: 0.3G
CARBOHYDRATE: 16G
PROTEIN: 1G
CHOLESTEROL: 0MG
SODIUM: 186MG

WARM CABBAGE SLAW

MAKES: 4 CUPS
WORKING TIME: 20 MINUTES
TOTAL TIME: 40 MINUTES

1 teaspoon olive oil
2 ounces Canadian bacon, diced
3 cloves garlic, minced
2 carrots, shredded
1 zucchini, slivered
4 cups coarsely shredded Savoy cabbage
2 tablespoons cider vinegar
¼ teaspoon salt
¼ teaspoon caraway seeds

1. In a large nonstick skillet, heat the oil until hot but not smoking over medium heat. Add the bacon and cook until the bacon is lightly crisped, about 2 minutes. Add the garlic and cook, stirring frequently, until the garlic is softened, about 1 minute.

2. Stir in the carrots and zucchini and cook until the vegetables are wilted, about 4 minutes. Add the cabbage, stirring to coat. Cover and cook until the cabbage is wilted, about 10 minutes.

3. Sprinkle the vinegar, salt, and caraway seeds over, stir well to combine, and cook, uncovered, just until the flavors are blended, about 3 minutes longer. Spoon the cabbage slaw into a medium bowl and serve.

Helpful hints: This dish can be prepared 1 day ahead—the flavor will improve—and then gently reheated in a skillet. You could also serve the slaw at room temperature.

VALUES ARE PER ½ CUP
FAT: 1G/27%
CALORIES: 39
SATURATED FAT: 0.2G
CARBOHYDRATE: 5G
PROTEIN: 3G
CHOLESTEROL: 4MG
SODIUM: 184MG

Zucchini and lean Canadian bacon are the surprises in this wilted slaw, nicely seasoned with cider vinegar and caraway seeds. We like this dish with turkey, chicken, or game birds, such as Cornish hens. Savoy cabbage is milder than regular green cabbage—look for a loose but full head, with crinkled pale to medium green leaves. Napa or regular cabbage can be substituted.

POTATO PANCAKES WITH APPLESAUCE

SERVES: 4
WORKING TIME: 25 MINUTES
TOTAL TIME: 55 MINUTES

3 Granny Smith apples, peeled, cored, and cut into ½-inch chunks

¾ cup thawed frozen apple juice concentrate

½ teaspoon vanilla

1½ pounds baking potatoes, peeled and shredded

¾ cup thinly sliced scallions

1 egg, lightly beaten

2 tablespoons flour

¾ teaspoon salt

½ teaspoon baking powder

¼ teaspoon freshly ground black pepper

2 teaspoons vegetable oil

1. In a medium saucepan, stir together the apples and juice concentrate and bring to a boil. Reduce to a simmer and cook, stirring frequently, until the apples are tender and the mixture is thickened but still chunky, about 15 minutes. Remove from the heat, stir in the vanilla, and set aside.

2. Meanwhile, preheat the oven to 400°. Spray a baking sheet with nonstick cooking spray. In a large bowl, combine the potatoes, scallions, egg, flour, salt, baking powder, and pepper and stir well.

3. Spray a large nonstick skillet with nonstick cooking spray, add 1 teaspoon of the oil, and heat until hot but not smoking over medium heat. Spoon ½ cup of the potato mixture into the pan, flattening the mixture slightly to form 1 pancake. Add as many more pancakes as will fit into the pan without crowding and cook until the pancakes are browned, about 3 minutes per side. Transfer to the prepared baking sheet. Repeat with the remaining 1 teaspoon oil and potato mixture.

4. Bake the pancakes for 5 minutes, or until the pancakes are cooked through and crisp. Serve the pancakes with the applesauce.

Helpful hints: You can bake the pancakes earlier in the day, and reheat them in a 300° oven. The applesauce can be made up to 1 day ahead, and is equally good served warm, chilled, or at room temperature.

FAT: 5G/14%
CALORIES: 309
SATURATED FAT: 0.8G
CARBOHYDRATE: 64G
PROTEIN: 5G
CHOLESTEROL: 53MG
SODIUM: 512G

These crispy, golden pancakes, flecked with bits of scallion, are sensational served at holiday time for brunch—perhaps luxuriously with a bit of reduced-fat sour cream and caviar—or with roasted meats or poultry. A double-apple applesauce, intensely flavored with apple juice concentrate, is an incredibly good go-with.

Hoppin' John

MAKES: 8 CUPS
WORKING TIME: 20 MINUTES
TOTAL TIME: 40 MINUTES

Commonly thought to bring good luck if eaten on New Year's Day, this zesty Southern side dish makes enough for lots of merrymakers.

1 cup long-grain rice

2 teaspoons olive oil

3 ounces Canadian bacon, coarsely chopped

2 medium onions, coarsely chopped

Two 10-ounce packages frozen black-eyed peas

2 tablespoons cider vinegar

1 teaspoon salt

½ teaspoon freshly ground black pepper

½ teaspoon hot pepper sauce

1. In a medium saucepan, combine the rice and 2 cups of water. Bring to a boil, reduce to a simmer, cover, and cook until the rice is tender, about 17 minutes. Set aside.

2. Meanwhile, in a large saucepan, heat the oil until hot but not smoking over medium heat. Add the bacon and cook until the bacon is lightly crisped, about 2 minutes. Add the onions and cook, stirring frequently, until the onions are softened, about 7 minutes.

3. Add the black-eyed peas and 2 cups of water and bring to a boil. Reduce to a simmer, cover, and cook until the peas are almost tender, about 10 minutes. Uncover and cook until the peas are tender and the water has evaporated, about 5 minutes longer.

4. Stir in the vinegar, salt, pepper, and hot pepper sauce. Add the rice, stir well to combine, and serve.

Helpful hint: Leftovers are delicious served chilled as a side salad—you may wish to add a bit more vinegar, hot pepper sauce, salt, and pepper since the rice and beans soak up some of the flavor.

VALUES ARE PER ½ CUP
FAT: 1G/1%
CALORIES: 113
SATURATED FAT: 0.3G
CARBOHYDRATE: 20G
PROTEIN: 5G
CHOLESTEROL: 3MG
SODIUM: 220MG

DESSERTS
4

*C*hocolate cake may seem too sinfully rich, but this egg-whites-only angel food cake has just one gram of fat. And to give you even more to enjoy, we've baked it in a springform rather than the usual tube pan. Garnish with raspberries and add chocolate curls by drawing a swivel-bladed vegetable peeler across the surface of a semisweet chocolate square.

CHOCOLATE ANGEL FOOD CAKE WITH RASPBERRY GLAZE

3 tablespoons unsweetened cocoa powder, preferably Dutch process

3 tablespoons boiling water

1 teaspoon vanilla

⅔ cup cake flour

1¼ cups plus 2 tablespoons sugar

1 cup egg whites (from 7 to 8 eggs)

1 teaspoon cream of tartar

¼ teaspoon salt

2 teaspoons unflavored gelatin

12-ounce package frozen raspberries (not in syrup), thawed

1. Preheat the oven to 350°. In a small bowl, stir together the cocoa, boiling water, and vanilla until smooth. On a sheet of wax paper, combine the flour and ¾ cup of the sugar. In a large bowl, with an electric mixer, beat the egg whites until foamy. Add the cream of tartar and salt and beat until soft peaks form. Gradually beat in 2 tablespoons of the sugar until stiff peaks form. Beat in the cocoa mixture. With a rubber spatula, gently fold in the flour mixture until just combined. Scrape the batter into an ungreased 9-inch springform pan, smoothing the top. Bake for 30 minutes, or until a toothpick inserted in the center comes out clean. Invert onto a prepared "rack" (see tip) and cool the cake completely in the pan.

2. Meanwhile, fill a large bowl with ice and water. Place ¼ cup of cold water in a small bowl, sprinkle the gelatin over, and let stand until dissolved, about 3 minutes. In a food processor, purée the raspberries and remaining ½ cup sugar until smooth. Strain the purée into a small saucepan, bring almost to a simmer over low heat, and stir in the dissolved gelatin until blended. Scrape the mixture into a medium bowl, place in the prepared bowl of ice and water, and let stand, stirring occasionally, until beginning to thicken, about 20 minutes.

3. With a metal spatula, loosen the cake from the side of the pan and remove the pan side. Place the cake on a plate, spoon the raspberry glaze on top, letting it drip down the sides, and serve.

FAT: 1G/2%
CALORIES: 211
SATURATED FAT: 0.2G
CARBOHYDRATE: 48G
PROTEIN: 5G
CHOLESTEROL: 0MG
SODIUM: 120MG

TIP

As is true of all angel food cakes, this cake cools upside down so it doesn't become compact. To fashion a cooling rack that will allow the cake to be suspended, invert 3 glasses of the same height on a flat surface, using the cake pan to space them so the rim of the pan will just rest on them.

OLD-FASHIONED ORANGE BUTTERMILK CAKE

SERVES: 8
WORKING TIME: 25 MINUTES
TOTAL TIME: 50 MINUTES PLUS COOLING TIME

This sunny-flavored single-layer cake, tangy with low-fat buttermilk and orange juice, will brighten any holiday table. For a simple garnish, we add orange slices, strips of orange zest, and fresh mint sprigs. Serve as a light finale for a lavish holiday dinner, or partner with cappuccino for a weekend open house.

1¼ cups cake flour
¾ teaspoon baking powder
¼ teaspoon baking soda
¼ teaspoon salt
¼ teaspoon ground ginger
1 whole egg
1 egg white
3 tablespoons unsalted butter
½ cup granulated sugar
⅓ cup firmly packed light brown sugar
2 teaspoons grated orange zest
2 tablespoons plus 2 teaspoons orange juice
⅔ cup low-fat (1.5%) buttermilk
½ cup confectioners' sugar

1. Preheat the oven to 350°. Spray an 8-inch round cake pan with nonstick cooking spray. Dust with flour, shaking off the excess. Line the bottom of the pan with a circle of wax paper. On a sheet of wax paper, stir together the flour, baking powder, baking soda, salt, and ginger. In a small bowl, whisk together the whole egg and egg white until well combined.

2. In a large bowl, with an electric mixer, beat the butter, granulated sugar, brown sugar, and orange zest until creamy. Gradually beat in the egg mixture, 1 teaspoon at a time, until light in texture, about 2 minutes. Beat in 2 tablespoons of the orange juice. With a rubber spatula, alternately fold in the flour mixture and the buttermilk, beginning and ending with the flour mixture, until just combined. Scrape the batter into the prepared pan, smoothing the top. Bake for 23 to 25 minutes, or until a toothpick inserted in the center comes out clean. Transfer to a wire rack and cool the cake in the pan for 10 minutes. Turn out onto the rack and cool completely.

3. In a small bowl, stir together the confectioners' sugar and remaining 2 teaspoons orange juice until smooth. Place the cake on a serving plate, spoon the glaze over, letting it drip down the sides, and serve.

Helpful hints: Substitute lemon zest and juice for the orange. This cake can be made 1 month ahead through step 2, wrapped tightly in plastic wrap, and frozen. Thaw in the refrigerator overnight, then glaze.

FAT: 6G/21%
CALORIES: 237
SATURATED FAT: 3.1G
CARBOHYDRATE: 44G
PROTEIN: 3G
CHOLESTEROL: 39MG
SODIUM: 182MG

DEEP-DISH APPLE COBBLER

SERVES: 8
WORKING TIME: 30 MINUTES
TOTAL TIME: 1 HOUR 10 MINUTES

1 cup plus 1 tablespoon flour

3 tablespoons plus ¾ cup sugar

1 teaspoon grated lemon zest

⅜ teaspoon salt

¼ teaspoon baking powder

3 tablespoons plus 2 teaspoons unsalted butter, cut up

¼ cup reduced-fat sour cream

6 Granny Smith apples, peeled, cored, and thinly sliced

2 teaspoons fresh lemon juice

¾ teaspoon cinnamon

⅛ teaspoon ground nutmeg

1. In a large bowl, stir together 1 cup of the flour, 3 tablespoons of the sugar, the lemon zest, ¼ teaspoon of the salt, and the baking powder. With a pastry blender or 2 knives, cut in 3 tablespoons of the butter until the mixture resembles coarse meal. Stir in the sour cream and 2 tablespoons of cold water. Add up to 1 tablespoon more water, 1 teaspoon at a time, until the dough just comes together. Pat into a disk, wrap in plastic wrap, and chill for 30 minutes.

2. Meanwhile, in a large bowl, combine the apples, remaining ¾ cup sugar, and remaining 1 tablespoon flour and toss well to coat. Add the lemon juice, cinnamon, nutmeg, and remaining ⅛ teaspoon salt and toss to combine. Spoon the mixture into a 9-inch deep-dish pie plate and dot the top with the remaining 2 teaspoons butter.

3. Preheat the oven to 425°. On a lightly floured board, pat the chilled dough into an 8-inch circle. Gently lift the dough and place on top of the filling. Place the cobbler on a baking sheet and bake for 15 minutes. Reduce the oven to 350° and bake for 25 minutes longer, or until the crust is golden brown. Transfer to a wire rack and cool the cobbler for 10 minutes, then serve.

Helpful hint: For a freshly baked dessert without fuss, assemble the filling in the pie plate and refrigerate it for up to 8 hours, then pat the top crust into a circle and refrigerate that as well. Just before you sit down to dinner, place the crust on top of the filling and pop it in the oven.

FAT: 7G/21%
CALORIES: 294
SATURATED FAT: 3.9G
CARBOHYDRATE: 58G
PROTEIN: 2G
CHOLESTEROL: 17MG
SODIUM: 120MG

This farmhouse favorite is a boon during the busy holiday season since it's easy to prepare, and can be served warm or at room temperature, depending on your timetable. The rich-tasting crust, made surprisingly low in fat with reduced-fat sour cream, is accented with a little lemon zest. Try serving the cobbler topped with vanilla nonfat yogurt, along with mugs of hot mulled cider.

The
seductive, silky texture
of this chiffon pie
is rendered even more
irresistible with a
lacing of heady
hazelnut liqueur.
The secret to the
remarkably low-fat
profile is the faux
whipped cream, made
with powdered milk.
Toast the pecans (this
brings out the flavor)
in a 350° oven on a
baking sheet with sides
for about ten minutes,
stirring occasionally.

PUMPKIN CHIFFON PIE WITH PECANS

SERVES: 8
WORKING TIME: 30 MINUTES
TOTAL TIME: 3 HOURS (INCLUDES CHILLING TIME)

*1 cup instant nonfat
powdered milk*

½ cup ice water

*1 cup zweiback crumbs (about
12 zweiback)*

1 cup graham cracker crumbs

3 tablespoons honey

2 tablespoons canola oil

2 envelopes unflavored gelatin

6 ounces nonfat cream cheese

*1 cup firmly packed dark
brown sugar*

1¼ teaspoons cinnamon

1 teaspoon vanilla

*2 cups canned solid-pack
pumpkin purée*

*2 tablespoons hazelnut liqueur
(optional)*

*¼ cup coarsely chopped pecans
or hazelnuts, toasted*

1. Preheat the oven to 350°. Place a small mixing bowl and beaters, the powdered milk, and ice water in the freezer to chill while you prepare the crust and filling. Spray a 9-inch pie plate with nonstick cooking spray. In a food processor, combine all the crumbs, the honey, and oil and process until blended. Scrape the mixture into the prepared pie plate and press firmly into the bottom and up the sides. Bake in the lower third of the oven for 8 to 10 minutes, or until the crust is just set. Transfer to a wire rack to cool.

2. Meanwhile, place ½ cup of cold water in a small bowl, and sprinkle the gelatin on top. Set the bowl over a small saucepan of simmering water and stir until the gelatin dissolves, about 3 minutes. Remove from the heat. In a food processor, combine the cream cheese, brown sugar, cinnamon, and vanilla and process until creamy. Add the pumpkin and liqueur and process until smooth. Add the dissolved gelatin and process until combined. Transfer to a medium bowl and refrigerate until the mixture is just beginning to set and is the texture of raw egg whites, about 45 minutes.

3. In the chilled mixing bowl, combine the powdered milk and ice water. With the chilled beaters, beat until very soft peaks form (see tip). With a rubber spatula, fold the milk mixture into the pumpkin mixture. Scrape the mixture into the crust and refrigerate until set, at least 1½ hours. Sprinkle the pecans on top and serve.

FAT: 8G/20%
CALORIES: 364
SATURATED FAT: 1G
CARBOHYDRATE: 64G
PROTEIN: 10G
CHOLESTEROL: 6MG
SODIUM: 280MG

GINGERBREAD WITH LEMON SAUCE

SERVES: 8
WORKING TIME: 20 MINUTES
TOTAL TIME: 50 MINUTES PLUS COOLING TIME

There's nothing like the aroma of gingerbread baking to bring on the holiday spirit—crystallized ginger gives this version a tasty twist.

1¼ cups cake flour

1¼ teaspoons ground ginger

1 teaspoon baking powder

½ teaspoon baking soda

½ teaspoon cinnamon

¼ teaspoon dry mustard

¼ teaspoon salt

3 tablespoons unsalted butter

½ cup firmly packed dark brown sugar

1 egg

2 tablespoons finely chopped crystallized ginger

2 teaspoons grated lemon zest

½ cup low-fat (1.5%) buttermilk

3 tablespoons molasses

3 tablespoons freshly brewed coffee

⅓ cup fresh lemon juice

¼ cup granulated sugar

¼ teaspoon ground nutmeg

1 teaspoon cornstarch mixed with 1 tablespoon water

1 tablespoon confectioners' sugar

1. Preheat the oven to 350°. Spray an 8-inch square cake pan with nonstick cooking spray. Dust the pan with flour, shaking off the excess. Line the bottom of the pan with a square of wax paper. On a sheet of wax paper, combine the flour, ground ginger, baking powder, baking soda, cinnamon, mustard, and salt.

2. In a large bowl, with an electric mixer, beat the butter and brown sugar until creamy. Beat in the egg, crystallized ginger, and zest. In a small bowl, mix the buttermilk, molasses, and coffee. With a rubber spatula, alternately fold the flour mixture and buttermilk mixture into the butter mixture, beginning and ending with the flour mixture, until just blended. Scrape into the prepared pan and smooth the top. Bake for 25 minutes, or until a toothpick inserted in the center comes out clean. Transfer to a wire rack and cool in the pan for 10 minutes. Turn out onto the rack; cool completely.

3. In a small saucepan, stir together the lemon juice, granulated sugar, 2 tablespoons of water, and nutmeg. Bring to a boil, reduce to a simmer, and cook until the sugar dissolves, about 2 minutes. Return to a boil, stir in the cornstarch mixture, and cook, stirring, until slightly thickened, about 1 minute. Place the cake on a plate, dust with the confectioners' sugar, and serve with the sauce.

Helpful hint: To garnish, place 2 ferns or a paper doily on the cake, dust with confectioners' sugar, then carefully lift off the pattern-maker.

FAT: 5G/20%
CALORIES: 237
SATURATED FAT: 3G
CARBOHYDRATE: 45G
PROTEIN: 3G
CHOLESTEROL: 39MG
SODIUM: 235MG

SERVES: 8
WORKING TIME: 30 MINUTES
TOTAL TIME: 30 MINUTES PLUS CHILLING TIME

½ cup plain nonfat yogurt

⅓ cup reduced-fat sour cream

½ cup honey

1 teaspoon grated lime zest

¼ cup fresh lime juice

3 cups cut fresh pineapple (½-inch chunks)

2 Granny Smith apples, cored and cut into ½-inch chunks

2 bananas, sliced

¾ cup halved seedless green grapes

¾ cup halved seedless red grapes

⅓ cup dried cherries or dried cranberries

½ cup coarsely chopped pecans

1. In a small bowl, whisk together the yogurt and sour cream. Whisk in 2 tablespoons of the honey and the lime zest and refrigerate until well chilled, about 1 hour.

2. In a large bowl, whisk together the lime juice and remaining 6 tablespoons honey until well combined. Add the pineapple, apples, bananas, grapes, cherries, and pecans, tossing gently to combine. Refrigerate until well chilled, about 1 hour.

3. Divide the fruit salad among 8 bowls, spoon the honey-yogurt dressing on top, and serve.

Helpful hints: For the best flavor and appearance, serve this salad soon after it's thoroughly chilled. Well-drained canned pineapple chunks can be substituted for the fresh and, if you prefer, orange will provide a softer tartness than lime.

FAT: 7G/24%
CALORIES: 241
SATURATED FAT: 1.1G
CARBOHYDRATE: 48G
PROTEIN: 3G
CHOLESTEROL: 4MG
SODIUM: 13MG

The tangy pineapple and lime-accented dressing of this fruit medley will awaken even the most party-tired palate.

LEMON POPPY SEED CAKE

SERVES: 12
WORKING TIME: 20 MINUTES
TOTAL TIME: 1 HOUR PLUS COOLING TIME

This is one of those moist cakes that tastes better a day after baking. Delicately textured, it makes a wonderful indulgence for a special brunch or dinner, or a quiet tea break in the afternoon.

Keep this recipe in mind when you need a hostess offering for a holiday party—it will always be welcomed.

3 tablespoons poppy seeds
2½ cups cake flour
1½ teaspoons baking powder
½ teaspoon baking soda
¼ teaspoon salt
¼ teaspoon ground allspice
2 whole eggs
1 egg white
6 tablespoons unsalted butter
1¾ cups sugar
1 tablespoon grated lemon zest
1½ cups low-fat (1.5%) buttermilk
¼ cup fresh lemon juice

1. Preheat the oven to 350°. Spray a 10-inch angel food or tube cake pan with nonstick cooking spray. Dust with flour, shaking off the excess. Spread the poppy seeds on a baking sheet with sides and bake for 4 minutes, or until lightly crisped. Set aside to cool.

2. On a sheet of wax paper, combine the flour, baking powder, baking soda, salt, allspice, and poppy seeds. In a small bowl, whisk together the eggs and egg white. In a large bowl, with an electric mixer, beat the butter, 1½ cups of the sugar, and the lemon zest until creamy. Gradually beat in the egg mixture, 1 teaspoon at a time, until light in texture. With a rubber spatula, alternately fold in the flour mixture and buttermilk, beginning and ending with the flour mixture, until just blended. Scrape the batter into the prepared pan, smoothing the top. Bake for 35 minutes, or until a toothpick inserted in the center comes out clean. Transfer to a wire rack.

3. In a small saucepan, stir together the lemon juice and remaining ¼ cup sugar. Bring to a boil over medium heat and cook, stirring constantly, until the sugar dissolves, about 2 minutes. With a fork, prick holes in the top of the cake and pour the hot syrup over the cake. Transfer to a wire rack and cool the cake in the pan for 10 minutes. Transfer to the rack and cool completely.

Helpful hint: For homemade buttermilk, combine 1½ tablespoons lemon juice and 1½ cups low-fat milk; let stand for 5 minutes to sour.

FAT: 8G/26%
CALORIES: 290
SATURATED FAT: 4.3G
CARBOHYDRATE: 50G
PROTEIN: 5G
CHOLESTEROL: 53MG
SODIUM: 191MG

CHOCOLATE-DIPPED FRUITS

SERVES: 4
WORKING TIME: 30 MINUTES
TOTAL TIME: 30 MINUTES PLUS SETTING TIME

4 ounces semisweet chocolate, coarsely chopped

1 teaspoon vegetable oil

1 green apple, cored, cut into 8 wedges, and patted dry

1 red apple, cored, cut into 8 wedges, and patted dry

1 cup whole strawberries, patted dry

¾ cup dried apricot halves

½ cup dried pear halves

1. In a small bowl set over, not in, a pan of simmering water, melt the chocolate, stirring frequently. Remove the bowl from over the pan, stir in the oil, and let cool slightly.

2. With a fork, spear each apple wedge and dip halfway into the melted chocolate. Place on a wire rack set over a sheet of wax paper. One at a time, by hand, dip the strawberries, apricots, and pears halfway into the melted chocolate and place on the rack. Let the fruits stand until the chocolate is firm. (If necessary, refrigerate for up to 30 minutes to help set the chocolate.) Divide the fruits among 4 dessert plates and serve.

Helpful hints: These are best served soon after the fruits have been dipped, since the chocolate will readily soften at room temperature. If serving on a buffet, arrange the fruits on a tray placed over a pan of ice water.

FAT: 10G/29%
CALORIES: 314
SATURATED FAT: 5.1G
CARBOHYDRATE: 62G
PROTEIN: 3G
CHOLESTEROL: 0MG
SODIUM: 7MG

What could be more tantalizing during the holidays than these delectable treats? Chocolate and fruit are one of those time- and taste-honored favorites, always popular, regardless of the season. Put a plate of these on a buffet table, and guests will make a beeline for them. Or serve with after-dinner cordials and coffee in front of the fire.

PEAR AND CRANBERRY SHORTCAKES

SERVES: 8
WORKING TIME: 25 MINUTES
TOTAL TIME: 1 HOUR PLUS COOLING TIME

This winter spin on a summer specialty is a delicious study in sweet and tart—cranberries and pears are bathed in a brandy-spiked sauce. We brush the tops of the buttermilk biscuits before baking with a little low-fat milk for a soft sheen. When the table is cleared, let guests retire to comfortable easy chairs in the living room, and serve the shortcakes with nut-flavored coffee.

1 teaspoon active dry yeast
¼ cup granulated sugar
2 cups all-purpose flour
1 tablespoon baking powder
½ teaspoon baking soda
½ teaspoon salt
3 tablespoons unsalted butter, cut up
¾ cup low-fat (1.5%) buttermilk
2 Bartlett pears, peeled, cored, and cut into 1-inch chunks
3 tablespoons brandy
12-ounce package fresh or frozen cranberries
¾ cup firmly packed light brown sugar
¼ teaspoon ground allspice
1 teaspoon cornstarch mixed with 1 tablespoon water
1 teaspoon vanilla
2 tablespoons low-fat (1%) milk
¼ cup reduced-fat sour cream

1. Place ¼ cup of warm water in a small bowl. Sprinkle the yeast and ½ teaspoon of the granulated sugar over and let stand until foamy, about 5 minutes. In a large bowl, combine the flour, all but 1 table-spoon of the granulated sugar, baking powder, baking soda, and salt. With a pastry blender or 2 knives, cut in 2 tablespoons plus 2 tea-spoons of the butter until the mixture resembles coarse meal. Stir the buttermilk into the yeast mixture, then stir into the dry ingredients until just blended. Cover; let rise in a warm place for 20 minutes.

2. Meanwhile, in a large nonstick skillet, cook the pears in the remain-ing 1 teaspoon butter over medium heat until lightly colored, about 2 minutes. Add the brandy and cook for 1 minute. Transfer to a bowl. Add the cranberries, brown sugar, allspice, and ½ cup of water to the pan and cook, stirring, until the berries pop, about 7 minutes. Stir in the cornstarch mixture and pears and bring to a boil. Cook, stirring, for 1 minute. Remove from the heat and stir in the vanilla.

3. Preheat the oven to 450°. On a lightly floured board, pat the dough into a rectangle about ½ inch thick. With a 3-inch biscuit cutter, cut out biscuits. Gather scraps, pat out, and cut out more biscuits. Transfer to a nonstick baking sheet, brush with the milk, sprinkle the remaining 1 tablespoon granulated sugar over, and bake for 14 minutes, or until crisp. Transfer to a wire rack to cool. Split the bis-cuits, place on 8 plates, fill with the fruit and sour cream, and serve.

FAT: 6G/16%
CALORIES: 347
SATURATED FAT: 3.5G
CARBOHYDRATE: 66G
PROTEIN: 5G
CHOLESTEROL: 16MG
SODIUM: 422MG

CITRUS-SCENTED RICE PUDDING

SERVES: 8
WORKING TIME: 15 MINUTES
TOTAL TIME: 1 HOUR

This soothing, old-fashioned dessert takes advantage of oranges and lemons—at their plentiful best during the holiday months.

⅔ cup long-grain rice

4 cups low-fat (1%) milk

⅔ cup firmly packed light brown sugar

Four 3 x ½-inch strips of orange zest

Four 3 x ½-inch strips of lemon zest

⅛ teaspoon salt

1 vanilla bean, split, or 1 teaspoon vanilla extract

½ cup evaporated low-fat milk

¼ cup golden raisins

1 teaspoon grated orange zest

1 teaspoon grated lemon zest

1. Heat a large pot of water to boiling over medium heat. Add the rice and cook for 10 minutes (the rice will not be tender). Drain well and set aside.

2. In a large heavy saucepan, combine the 4 cups milk, brown sugar, orange and lemon zest strips, salt, and vanilla bean (if using the vanilla extract, do not add it now). Heat over medium-low heat just until small bubbles appear around the edges of the pan. Stir in the rice. Cover and cook, stirring occasionally, until the rice is tender and the mixture is creamy, about 45 minutes.

3. Remove the pudding from the heat. Remove and discard the orange and lemon zest strips. Remove the vanilla bean and save it for another use (see the hint, below). If using the vanilla extract, stir it into the pudding now along with the evaporated milk and raisins. Spoon the rice pudding into 8 bowls, sprinkle the grated orange and lemon zest on top, and serve warm.

Helpful hints: Rice pudding is also good served chilled, and can be prepared up to 1 day ahead. Reuse the vanilla bean to make vanilla sugar; rinse the bean well, dry, and place it in your sugar canister to perfume the sugar. Use the vanilla sugar stirred into hot drinks, or sprinkled over cereal, French toast, or fruit salads.

FAT: 2G/7%
CALORIES: 208
SATURATED FAT: 0.8G
CARBOHYDRATE: 42G
PROTEIN: 6G
CHOLESTEROL: 7MG
SODIUM: 121MG

Holiday Honey Cake

SERVES: 12
WORKING TIME: 25 MINUTES
TOTAL TIME: 1 HOUR PLUS COOLING TIME

2¼ cups cake flour

2 teaspoons baking powder

1 teaspoon baking soda

1 teaspoon cinnamon

¾ teaspoon salt

½ teaspoon ground cardamom

¼ teaspoon ground cloves

¼ cup unsweetened cocoa powder, preferably Dutch process

1 tablespoon grated orange zest

2 tablespoons plus 1½ cups orange juice

4 eggs, separated

1¼ cups granulated sugar

½ cup honey

2 tablespoons fresh lemon juice

1 tablespoon cornstarch mixed with ¼ cup water

1 teaspoon confectioners' sugar

1. Preheat the oven to 325°. Spray a 9-inch tube pan with nonstick cooking spray. On a sheet of wax paper, combine the flour, baking powder, baking soda, cinnamon, ½ teaspoon of the salt, the cardamom, and cloves. In a small bowl, stir together the cocoa, ⅓ cup of water, orange zest, and 2 tablespoons of the orange juice.

2. In a large bowl, with an electric mixer, beat the egg yolks, ¾ cup of the granulated sugar, and the honey until pale and thick. Beat in the cocoa mixture. With a rubber spatula, gently fold in the flour mixture. In a separate mixing bowl, with clean beaters, beat the egg whites with the remaining ¼ teaspoon salt until stiff peaks form. Stir one-fourth of the egg whites into the batter to lighten, then gently fold in the remaining whites. Scrape into the prepared pan, smoothing the top. Bake for 40 minutes, or until the cake is lightly browned. Transfer to a wire rack and cool the cake in the pan for 10 minutes. Turn out onto the rack to cool completely.

3. Place the cake on a serving plate. In a small saucepan, combine the lemon juice, remaining 1½ cups orange juice, and remaining ½ cup granulated sugar. Bring to a boil over medium heat and cook, stirring constantly, until the sugar dissolves, about 2 minutes. Stir in the cornstarch mixture and cook, stirring constantly, until the sauce is slightly thickened, about 1 minute. Dust the cake with the confectioners' sugar and serve with the sauce.

FAT: 2G/8%
CALORIES: 248
SATURATED FAT: 0.7G
CARBOHYDRATE: 55G
PROTEIN: 4G
CHOLESTEROL: 71MG
SODIUM: 347MG

A romatic with sweet spices, this cake is surprisingly light—and tempting after even the heartiest holiday meal.

Decadently fudgy and moist, this cake, spiked with a touch of rum, will elicit murmurs of delight from the most demanding dessert connoisseurs. And as the name implies, a slightly concave top is to be expected. Garnish with whole strawberries and arrange the cake as the centerpiece for a holiday dessert buffet.

Fallen Chocolate Mousse Cake

Serves: 8
Working time: 20 minutes
Total time: 45 minutes plus cooling time

1 cup plain nonfat yogurt

¾ cup granulated sugar

½ cup unsweetened cocoa powder, preferably Dutch process

¼ cup firmly packed light brown sugar

1 teaspoon cinnamon

¼ teaspoon ground nutmeg

1 tablespoon dark rum

2 ounces semisweet chocolate, coarsely chopped and melted (see tip)

2 eggs, separated

6 tablespoons flour

2 egg whites

¼ teaspoon cream of tartar

¼ teaspoon salt

2 teaspoons confectioners' sugar

1. Preheat the oven to 375°. Spray an 8½-inch springform pan with nonstick cooking spray. Line the bottom of the pan with a circle of wax paper. In a small bowl, stir together the yogurt and 2 tablespoons of the granulated sugar. Refrigerate until serving time.

2. In a medium bowl, stir together ½ cup of the granulated sugar, the cocoa powder, brown sugar, cinnamon, and nutmeg. Stir in ⅓ cup of hot water, the rum, and half of the melted chocolate. In a small bowl, with a fork, lightly beat the egg yolks. Stir in one-quarter of the warm cocoa mixture, then stir the yolk mixture back into the cocoa mixture. With a rubber spatula, stir in the flour.

3. In a large bowl, with an electric mixer, beat the 4 egg whites until foamy. Add the cream of tartar and salt and beat until soft peaks form. Gradually beat in the remaining 2 tablespoons granulated sugar until stiff peaks form. Stir ½ cup of the egg whites into the batter to lighten, then gently fold in the remaining whites. Scrape the batter into the prepared pan, smoothing the top. Bake for 25 minutes, or until a toothpick inserted in the center comes out just clean. Transfer to a wire rack to cool completely.

4. With a metal spatula, loosen the cake from the side of the pan and remove the pan side. Place the cake on a plate, dust with the confectioners' sugar, and drizzle the remaining melted chocolate on top. Serve the sweetened yogurt on the side.

Fat: 4g/18%
Calories: 213
Saturated Fat: 2.1g
Carbohydrate: 41g
Protein: 6g
Cholesterol: 54mg
Sodium: 124mg

SUGAR COOKIES

MAKES: 2½ DOZEN
WORKING TIME: 25 MINUTES
TOTAL TIME: 35 MINUTES PLUS CHILLING TIME

These delicate sugar cookies, flavored with a hint of lemon and vanilla, are clearly destined for an afternoon tea party. And they are equally appropriate as a light finish to a many-course holiday meal. For the best flavor and lightest texture, serve them warm from the oven. This is the occasion to break out your favorite holiday cookie cutters.

1½ cups flour
1¼ teaspoons baking powder
¼ teaspoon salt
3 tablespoons unsalted butter
¼ cup reduced-fat sour cream
1 cup granulated sugar
1½ teaspoons grated lemon zest
1 teaspoon vanilla
2 egg whites
2 tablespoons colored sugar

1. On a sheet of wax paper, combine the flour, baking powder, and salt. In a large bowl, with an electric mixer, beat the butter and sour cream until creamy. Beat in the granulated sugar, lemon zest, and vanilla. Beat in the egg whites until light and creamy. With a wooden spoon, stir in the flour mixture. Wrap the dough in plastic wrap and refrigerate until firm enough to roll out, about 2 hours.

2. Preheat the oven to 400°. On a lightly floured board, roll the dough to a ¼-inch thickness. With a 2-inch round cookie cutter or several decorative cookie cutters, cut out cookies. Gather the scraps, reroll, and cut out more cookies. Place the cookies, 1 inch apart, on 2 ungreased baking sheets, then sprinkle the colored sugar on top, gently pressing into the dough. Bake for 7 minutes, or until the cookies are just set and the edges are lightly browned. Place on a festive plate and serve.

Helpful hints: To impress your guests with just-baked cookies, place the cut-out dough on the baking sheets in the refrigerator before dinner. Then when clearing the table for dessert, just pop the cookies into the oven. For convenience, prepare the dough up to 1 month ahead through step 1 and store in the freezer. Thaw at room temperature for about 2 hours before rolling and cutting into cookies.

VALUES ARE PER COOKIE
FAT: 1G/19%
CALORIES: 68
SATURATED FAT: 0.9G
CARBOHYDRATE: 13G
PROTEIN: 1G
CHOLESTEROL: 4MG
SODIUM: 42MG

APPLE-CRANBERRY CRUMBLE

SERVES: 8
WORKING TIME: 35 MINUTES
TOTAL TIME: 1 HOUR

1 cup granulated sugar

3 tablespoons cornstarch

12-ounce package fresh or frozen cranberries

3 McIntosh apples, peeled, cored, and cut into ½-inch chunks

½ cup apple juice

2 teaspoons vanilla

1½ teaspoons grated lemon zest

⅛ teaspoon freshly ground black pepper

½ cup old-fashioned rolled oats

6 tablespoons firmly packed light brown sugar

6 tablespoons flour

2 tablespoons coarsely chopped pecans

3½ tablespoons unsalted butter, cut up

1. Preheat the oven to 375°. Spray a 9-inch pie plate with nonstick cooking spray. In a small bowl, stir together ½ cup of the granulated sugar and the cornstarch.

2. In a medium saucepan, stir together the cranberries and remaining ½ cup granulated sugar. Cook, stirring frequently, over medium heat until the sugar dissolves and the berries pop slightly, about 5 minutes. Stir in the cornstarch mixture, bring to a boil, and cook, stirring constantly, until the mixture is slightly thickened, about 1 minute. Remove from the heat and stir in the apples, apple juice, vanilla, lemon zest, and pepper. Spoon the apple mixture into the prepared pie plate.

3. In a medium bowl, stir together the oats, brown sugar, flour, and pecans. With a pastry blender or 2 knives, cut in the butter until coarse crumbs form. Sprinkle the crumbs over the apple mixture, place the pie plate on a baking sheet, and bake for 25 minutes, or until the filling is bubbly and the topping is golden brown.

Helpful hints: Walnuts or hazelnuts can be substituted for the pecans. This is the type of dessert that can be easily readied earlier in the day and refrigerated. To serve, simply bring to room temperature, or reheat in a low oven or in the microwave at half power, rotating the dish occasionally.

FAT: 7G/20%
CALORIES: 304
SATURATED FAT: 3.3G
CARBOHYDRATE: 61G
PROTEIN: 2G
CHOLESTEROL: 14MG
SODIUM: 6MG

J ust a pinch of black pepper accents this classic winter dessert. And we've added a little richness to the crumbly oat topping— a sprinkling of chopped pecans. For a sit-down dinner, prepare the recipe in small ramekins, and set out a bowl of sweetened nonfat yogurt for dolloping. This is equally good served warm or at room temperature.

POACHED PEARS WITH CARAMEL SAUCE

SERVES: 4
WORKING TIME: 15 MINUTES
TOTAL TIME: 40 MINUTES PLUS CHILLING TIME

These pears, infused with a spicy flavor, are lusciously teamed with a caramel sauce made with evaporated low-fat milk—not cream.

1¼ cups dry white wine
⅓ cup granulated sugar
1 bay leaf
8 black peppercorns
½ teaspoon ground ginger
¼ teaspoon cinnamon
⅛ teaspoon ground allspice
4 ripe Bartlett pears, stems left on, peeled and cored
3 tablespoons firmly packed light brown sugar
1 tablespoon light corn syrup
½ cup evaporated low-fat milk

1. In a medium saucepan just large enough to hold the pears lying on their sides, combine the wine, granulated sugar, ½ cup of water, the bay leaf, peppercorns, ginger, cinnamon, and allspice. Bring to a boil over medium heat, reduce to a simmer, and add the pears. Place a sheet of wax paper on top and poach, turning occasionally, until the pears are tender, about 20 minutes. (The poaching time will vary depending on the ripeness of the pears.) Transfer the pears and poaching liquid to a bowl and refrigerate until well chilled, at least 1 hour.

2. In a small saucepan, stir together the brown sugar and corn syrup. Stir in the evaporated milk. Bring to a boil over medium heat, reduce to a simmer, and cook until the sauce is just slightly thickened, about 5 minutes. Let cool to room temperature.

3. Spoon about half of the caramel sauce into 4 dessert dishes, dividing evenly. With a slotted spoon, place 1 pear in each dish, discarding the poaching liquid in the bowl. Spoon the remaining caramel sauce on top and serve.

Helpful hint: Both the pears and the sauce can be prepared 1 day ahead and refrigerated separately. Let the sauce stand at room temperature for about 1 hour before serving, or very gently rewarm.

FAT: 1G/4%
CALORIES: 266
SATURATED FAT: 0G
CARBOHYDRATE: 60G
PROTEIN: 3G
CHOLESTEROL: 5MG
SODIUM: 47MG

CHOCOLATE BREAD PUDDING

SERVES: 8
WORKING TIME: 15 MINUTES
TOTAL TIME: 40 MINUTES

6 slices cinnamon-raisin bread,
lightly toasted

3 tablespoons unsweetened
cocoa powder, preferably Dutch
process

2 cups low-fat (1%) milk

⅓ cup firmly packed light
brown sugar

2 teaspoons cornstarch

1 teaspoon grated orange zest

⅛ teaspoon ground allspice

⅛ teaspoon ground nutmeg

2 whole eggs

3 egg whites

2 teaspoons confectioners' sugar

3 tablespoons chocolate syrup

1. Preheat the oven to 350°. Spray a shallow 11 x 7-inch baking dish with nonstick cooking spray. Arrange the bread in the prepared dish, overlapping the slices slightly.

2. Place the cocoa powder in a small bowl, and stir in ¼ cup of the milk until smooth. Stir in the remaining 1¾ cups milk, the brown sugar, cornstarch, orange zest, allspice, and nutmeg. Whisk in the whole eggs and egg whites until well combined. Pour the mixture over the bread, cover with foil, and bake for 25 minutes, or until the pudding is just set.

3. Dust the pudding with the confectioners' sugar, drizzle the chocolate syrup on top, and serve.

Helpful hints: Experiment with other kinds of bread, such as challah or Portuguese sweet bread. The bread pudding can be prepared earlier in the day and refrigerated, then served deliciously chilled.

FAT: 3G/17%
CALORIES: 169
SATURATED FAT: 1.2G
CARBOHYDRATE: 30G
PROTEIN: 7G
CHOLESTEROL: 56MG
SODIUM: 160MG

read pudding always conjures up holiday kitchens, full of good aromas. Ours is rich, chocolaty, and delicious.

115

Surprise and delight your holiday guests with this sophisticated Champagne dessert— a refreshing granita whose coarse-crystalled ice explodes with citrus flavor. And what's even better, there's no fat.

LEMON CHAMPAGNE GRANITA

SERVES: 8
WORKING TIME: 15 MINUTES
TOTAL TIME: 3 HOURS 15 MINUTES (INCLUDES FREEZING TIME)

1 cup sugar
2 teaspoons grated lemon zest
2 cups fresh lemon juice
½ cup Champagne

1. In a medium nonaluminum saucepan, combine the sugar and 1 cup of water. Bring to a rolling boil over high heat, stirring to dissolve the sugar. Remove from the heat and stir in ¾ cup of water, the lemon zest, lemon juice, and Champagne.

2. Pour the mixture into a shallow 1½-quart plastic or glass container and freeze until frozen around the edges, about 2 hours.

3. Stir the mixture by bringing the frozen bits from the bottom and sides of the container toward the center (see tip). Continue to freeze until the mixture is no longer liquid, stirring every 10 minutes as directed, about 1 hour longer. Stir the granita well, spoon into 8 well-chilled dessert dishes, and serve.

Helpful hints: To get the needed amount of lemon juice, you'll need about 10 or 11 lemons. You can prepare the granita 1 week ahead, but transfer it to a freezer container, packing it well. Let soften slightly at room temperature if the mixture has frozen too hard, so the crystals can begin to separate.

TIP

To keep the granita coarsely textured, and to ensure that it freezes evenly, stir it every 10 minutes, bringing the frozen bits from the bottom and sides of the pan toward the center.

FAT: 0G/0%
CALORIES: 122
SATURATED FAT: 0G
CARBOHYDRATE: 30G
PROTEIN: 0G
CHOLESTEROL: 0MG
SODIUM: 2MG

STRAWBERRY-TOPPED LEMON CHEESECAKE

SERVES: 12
WORKING TIME: 25 MINUTES
TOTAL TIME: 1 HOUR 35 MINUTES PLUS COOLING TIME

1 cup zweiback crumbs (about 12 zweiback)

1 cup graham cracker crumbs

2 tablespoons honey

1 tablespoon canola oil

2½ cups low-fat (1%) cottage cheese

11 ounces reduced-fat cream cheese (Neufchâtel)

3 tablespoons flour

1 tablespoon grated lemon zest

2 teaspoons vanilla

1¼ cups sugar

2 whole eggs

2 egg whites

1 cup halved strawberries, stems left on if desired

2 tablespoons strawberry jelly

1. Preheat the oven to 350°. In a medium bowl, stir together all the crumbs, the honey, and oil. Firmly press the mixture into the bottom and halfway up the sides of a 9-inch springform pan.

2. In a food processor or blender, combine the cottage cheese, cream cheese, flour, lemon zest, and vanilla and purée until smooth. Add the sugar, whole eggs, and egg whites and process until just combined. Scrape the batter into the crust and bake for 50 minutes, or until the cheesecake is still a little jiggly in the center but set around the edges. Turn off the oven, prop the oven door open, and let the cheesecake cool in the oven for 30 minutes. Transfer to a wire rack to cool completely.

3. With a metal spatula, loosen the cheesecake from the side of the pan and remove the pan side. Place the cake on a plate and arrange the strawberries in the center. In a small saucepan, warm the jelly over low heat until melted, brush over the strawberries, and serve.

Helpful hints: Other berries—such as raspberries or blueberries—could be nicely substituted for the strawberries. The cheesecake can be prepared up to 1 day ahead and refrigerated.

Grandly finish a holiday dinner with this spectacular cheesecake, and do so confidently, knowing its appearance and taste belie its low-fat nature—the tricks are using low-fat cottage cheese and reduced-fat cream cheese.

FAT: 10G/29%
CALORIES: 310
SATURATED FAT: 4.7G
CARBOHYDRATE: 43G
PROTEIN: 12G
CHOLESTEROL: 58MG
SODIUM: 392MG

HAZELNUT MACAROONS

MAKES: 3 DOZEN
WORKING TIME: 25 MINUTES
TOTAL TIME: 40 MINUTES

Best served the same day they are baked, these lovely little cookies are ideal for dunking into coffee or tea—or Champagne.

1¼ cups old-fashioned rolled oats

3 ounces shelled hazelnuts

1 cup sugar

2 tablespoons plain dried bread crumbs

2 egg whites

½ teaspoon vanilla

18 candied cherries, halved

1. Preheat the oven to 350°. Spread the oats on a baking sheet with sides. Spread the hazelnuts on a separate baking sheet with sides. Bake the oats and hazelnuts for 15 minutes, shaking the baking sheets occasionally, or until the oats are crisp and fragrant and the hazelnut skins begin to flake. Set aside to cool slightly. Keep the oven on.

2. Place the hazelnuts in a kitchen towel, fold the towel over the nuts, and vigorously rub to remove most of the skins. In a food processor, combine the hazelnuts and sugar and process until finely ground. Add the oats and process until combined. Add the bread crumbs, egg whites, and vanilla and process until well combined.

3. Line the same 2 baking sheets with foil. With dampened hands, form the hazelnut mixture into about 36 walnut-sized balls and place, 1 inch apart, on the prepared baking sheets. Press a cherry half into the center of each, gently flatten, and bake for 17 minutes, or until the macaroons are set and very lightly browned around the edges. Cool on the baking sheets for 5 minutes. Peel the macaroons off the foil and transfer to a wire rack to cool completely. Place on a plate and serve.

Helpful hint: You can substitute almonds for the hazelnuts.

VALUES ARE PER COOKIE
FAT: 2G/27%
CALORIES: 56
SATURATED FAT: 0.1G
CARBOHYDRATE: 10G
PROTEIN: 1G
CHOLESTEROL: 0MG
SODIUM: 7MG

HOMEMADE GIFTS

5

CRANBERRY-ORANGE BREAD

MAKES: 3 MINI-LOAVES
WORKING TIME: 25 MINUTES
TOTAL TIME: 1 HOUR 10 MINUTES PLUS COOLING TIME

*F*lecked with cranberries and pecans, these tempting mini-loaves are deliciously flavored with tangy buttermilk and spicy-hot crystallized ginger. Wrap in colored cellophane, tie with ribbon, and they're all set for a hostess gift or for distributing to co-workers. Serve for an afternoon tea break with reduced-fat cream cheese or a favorite jam.

3 cups flour

1½ teaspoons grated orange zest

1 teaspoon baking powder

1 teaspoon baking soda

1 teaspoon salt

1 whole egg

2 egg whites

½ cup granulated sugar

½ cup firmly packed light brown sugar

3 tablespoons vegetable oil

¾ cup low-fat (1.5%) buttermilk

½ cup orange juice

1½ cups coarsely chopped fresh or frozen cranberries

⅔ cup coarsely chopped pecans, toasted

3 tablespoons coarsely chopped crystallized ginger

1. Preheat the oven to 350°. Spray three 5½ x 3-inch mini-loaf pans with nonstick cooking spray. Dust with flour, shaking off the excess. In a large bowl, stir together the flour, orange zest, baking powder, baking soda, and salt.

2. In a large bowl, with an electric mixer, beat the egg, egg whites, granulated sugar, and brown sugar until light and fluffy. Beat in the oil until well combined. With a wooden spoon, stir in the buttermilk and orange juice. Stir in the flour mixture until just combined. Gently stir in the cranberries, pecans, and ginger.

3. Divide the batter among the prepared pans and bake for 45 minutes, or until a toothpick inserted in the center comes out clean. Transfer to a wire rack and cool the loaves in the pans for 10 minutes. Turn out onto the rack and cool completely.

Helpful hints: If you are using frozen cranberries, chop them in a food processor so you don't have to thaw them. You can prepare two batches (or more) of this bread, but make the recipe twice, or as many times as desired—don't just double the ingredients. (If you mix too much batter at once, the bread may be dense and tough.) The loaves can be made up to 3 months ahead, wrapped tightly in plastic wrap, and frozen.

VALUES ARE PER ½-INCH SLICE
FAT: 3G/27%
CALORIES: 107
SATURATED FAT: 0.4G
CARBOHYDRATE: 18G
PROTEIN: 2G
CHOLESTEROL: 7MG
SODIUM: 130MG

CHOCOLATE CHIP MERINGUES

MAKES: 2 DOZEN
WORKING TIME: 20 MINUTES
TOTAL TIME: 1 HOUR 20 MINUTES PLUS STANDING TIME

4 egg whites
1 cup sugar
½ teaspoon vanilla
¼ teaspoon cream of tartar
Pinch of salt
*6 tablespoons miniature
semisweet chocolate chips*

1. Preheat the oven to 250°. Line 2 baking sheets with parchment paper or spray the sheets with nonstick cooking spray and dust with flour, shaking off the excess.

2. In a large bowl, with an electric mixer, beat the egg whites until soft peaks form. Gradually beat in ½ cup of the sugar, 1 tablespoon at a time. Beat in the vanilla, cream of tartar, and salt. Gradually beat in the remaining ½ cup sugar, 1 tablespoon at a time, until the sugar dissolves and stiff peaks form, about 8 minutes. With a wooden spoon, gently fold in the chocolate chips.

3. Drop the mixture by large tablespoonfuls, 2 inches apart, on the prepared baking sheets and bake for 1 hour, or until the meringues are set. Turn off the oven, prop the oven door open, and let the meringues stand in the oven until dry, about 1 hour.

Helpful hints: Avoid making meringues on a humid day since the finished cookies will absorb moisture from the air, making them gummy. For best results, be sure the whites are sufficiently beaten and the sugar is completely dissolved (rub a small amount of the mixture between your fingers; it should not feel grainy). Give as a gift soon after baking, and store in an airtight container at room temperature for up to 1 week.

VALUES ARE PER COOKIE
FAT: 1G/14%
CALORIES: 48
SATURATED FAT: 0.4G
CARBOHYDRATE: 10G
PROTEIN: 1G
CHOLESTEROL: 0MG
SODIUM: 15MG

Present these wonderful treats in a fancy holiday tin. And give the recipients ample warning—once they sample them, these lighter-than-air meringues may be gone in a matter of minutes. Served with coffee or espresso, they make a sweet finish for any holiday meal. Be sure to bake the meringues for the full amount of time so the insides are sufficiently dry.

PEPPER JELLY

MAKES: 5 HALF-PINTS
WORKING TIME: 20 MINUTES
TOTAL TIME: 20 MINUTES

Nicely spiked with jalapeño peppers, chili powder, and cayenne pepper, this jelly will find innumerable serving uses during the holiday season. It is delicious spread on crackers with reduced-fat cream cheese as an hors d'oeuvre, spooned on toasted bagels or hot biscuits with brunch, or as a condiment with roast poultry or beef.

2 red bell peppers, quartered
1 green bell pepper, quartered
⅓ cup pickled jalapeño peppers, seeded and diced
1¼ cups distilled white vinegar
½ cup minced scallions
1¾-ounce package powdered pectin
1¼ teaspoons mild chili powder
¾ teaspoon salt
¼ teaspoon cayenne pepper
5¼ cups sugar

1. Wash 5 half-pint jars and lids in hot soapy water and rinse well. Keep the lids and bands in hot water. To sterilize, place the jars, right-side up, on the rack in a water bath canner (or in a large saucepan), cover with hot water by 1 inch, and then boil for 10 minutes. Keep the jars in the hot water until ready to use.

2. In a food processor, combine the bell peppers and jalapeño peppers and process until puréed (the mixture will not be completely smooth).

3. In a large nonaluminum saucepan, stir together the pepper purée, vinegar, scallions, pectin, chili powder, salt, and cayenne. Cook over medium heat, stirring occasionally, until the mixture comes to a rolling boil that cannot be stirred down, about 4 minutes. Stir in the sugar and boil for 1 minute longer, skimming any foam that rises to the surface.

4. Drain the sterilized jars. Ladle the jelly through a sterilized funnel into the jars up to ¼ inch from the top, seal the jars, and refrigerate for up to 3 weeks. For longer storage, or if planning to keep unrefrigerated, process the filled jars in a boiling water bath for 5 minutes (p. 10).

Helpful hint: If you'd like a jelly with less heat, substitute a 4-ounce can of mild green chilies for the pickled jalapeños.

VALUES ARE PER 1 TABLESPOON
FAT: 0G/0%
CALORIES: 54
SATURATED FAT: 0G
CARBOHYDRATE: 14G
PROTEIN: 0G
CHOLESTEROL: 0MG
SODIUM: 31MG

BUTTERSCOTCH SAUCE

MAKES: 6 HALF-PINTS
WORKING TIME: 15 MINUTES
TOTAL TIME: 15 MINUTES

*4 cups firmly packed dark
brown sugar
2 cups light corn syrup
2 tablespoons unsalted butter
2 cups evaporated low-fat milk
1 teaspoon vanilla
½ teaspoon salt*

1. Wash 6 half-pint jars and lids in hot soapy water and rinse well. Keep the lids and bands in hot water. To sterilize, place the jars, right-side up, in a large saucepan, cover with hot water by 1 inch, and then boil for 10 minutes. Keep the jars in the hot water until ready to use.

2. In a large saucepan, combine the brown sugar and corn syrup. Cook over medium-low heat, stirring occasionally, until the sugar dissolves, about 6 minutes.

3. Remove the mixture from the heat and stir in the butter until melted. Stir in the evaporated milk, vanilla, and salt until combined. Drain the sterilized jars. Pour the butterscotch sauce into the jars, seal the jars, and refrigerate for up to 1 week. This sauce cannot be processed in a boiling water bath.

Helpful hint: Heat the brown sugar and corn syrup over medium-low heat to avoid scorching the sugar.

VALUES ARE PER 1 TABLESPOON
FAT: 0.3G/5%
CALORIES: 61
SATURATED FAT: 0.1G
CARBOHYDRATE: 15G
PROTEIN: 0G
CHOLESTEROL: 1MG
SODIUM: 29MG

Our rendition of this classic dessert sauce tastes just as rich as the ice cream parlor favorite—but we've cut way back on the fat by using evaporated low-fat milk. Present it in heavy, glass-topped mason jars, wrapped in decorative foil paper. Spoon chilled or warm over frozen yogurt, toasted slices of fat-free pound cake, or even a bowl of mixed fresh berries.

Butterscotch Sauce
4 cups brown sugar
2 cups corn syrup
2 T unsalted butter
2 cups low-fat evap milk
1 t vanilla
1/2 t salt

sauce

& syrup.

Here's a low-fat version of a chocolate cookie classic, subtly flavored with orange, to add to your holiday favorites. These thumbprints only seem sinfully rich—the healthy secret's in reduced-fat sour cream. Take them along to a party in an attractive tin. Make a batch for yourself as well—they're ideal to serve with coffee to unexpected holiday drop-ins.

130

Chocolate Jam Thumbprints

MAKES: 2½ DOZEN
WORKING TIME: 20 MINUTES
TOTAL TIME: 35 MINUTES

1¾ cups flour

¼ cup unsweetened cocoa powder, preferably Dutch process

1 teaspoon baking powder

¼ teaspoon baking soda

¼ teaspoon salt

⅓ cup reduced-fat sour cream

2 tablespoons unsalted butter

1 cup sugar

1½ teaspoons grated orange zest

1 teaspoon vanilla

2 egg whites

2½ tablespoons red currant jelly

1. Preheat the oven to 400°. On a sheet of wax paper, stir together the flour, cocoa, baking powder, baking soda, and salt. In a large bowl, with an electric mixer, beat the sour cream and butter until creamy. Beat in the sugar, orange zest, and vanilla until creamy. Beat in the egg whites until light and creamy. With a wooden spoon, stir in the flour mixture until just combined.

2. With dampened hands, pinch off walnut-size pieces of the dough and roll into 30 balls. Place the balls, 1 inch apart, on 2 ungreased baking sheets. With your thumb, make an indentation in the center of each ball and spoon about ¼ teaspoon of the jelly into each thumbprint (see tip). Bake for 10 minutes, or until the cookies are set and the edges are barely crisp. Transfer to a wire rack to cool.

Helpful hints: If you are making several batches of cookies, repeat the recipe rather than doubling or tripling the ingredients in a single batch. To pack for gift-giving, separate each layer of cookies with a sheet of wax paper to keep the jelly in place. Store the thumbprints in an airtight container at room temperature for up to 1 week.

TIP

Place the jelly in a small dish and, with a teaspoon, spoon the jelly into the thumbprint in each cookie.

VALUES ARE PER COOKIE
FAT: 1G/16%
CALORIES: 71
SATURATED FAT: 0.7G
CARBOHYDRATE: 14G
PROTEIN: 1G
CHOLESTEROL: 3MG
SODIUM: 49MG

PICKLED VEGETABLES ITALIANO

MAKES: 4 PINTS
WORKING TIME: 35 MINUTES
TOTAL TIME: 35 MINUTES

1 quart cider vinegar

1 cup sugar

2 tablespoons black peppercorns

2 tablespoons pickling spice

1 teaspoon salt

4 cloves garlic, peeled

2 bay leaves

4 cups small cauliflower florets

1 pound carrots, thinly sliced on the diagonal

1 pound green beans, halved crosswise

2 red bell peppers, cut into wide strips

2 yellow bell peppers, cut into wide strips

4 sprigs of fresh dill

1. Wash 4 pint jars and lids in hot soapy water and rinse well. Keep the lids and bands in hot water. To sterilize, place the jars, right-side up, on the rack in a water bath canner (or in a large saucepan), cover with hot water by 1 inch, and then boil for 10 minutes. Keep the jars in the hot water until ready to use.

2. In a medium nonaluminum saucepan, combine the vinegar, sugar, peppercorns, pickling spice, salt, garlic, and bay leaves. Bring to a boil over high heat. Reduce the heat to medium and simmer until the flavors have blended, about 10 minutes. Discard the garlic and bay leaves. Meanwhile, in a large stockpot of boiling water, cook the cauliflower, carrots, green beans, and bell peppers for 2 to 3 minutes to blanch (the vegetables should still be quite crisp). Drain, rinse under cold water, and drain again thoroughly.

3. Drain the sterilized jars. Divide the vegetables among the jars, packing to fit. Place 1 dill sprig in each jar. Pour the hot vinegar mixture over the vegetables up to ½ inch from the top, seal the jars, and refrigerate for up to 3 weeks. For longer storage, or if planning to keep unrefrigerated, process the filled jars in a boiling water bath for 15 minutes (p. 10).

Helpful hint: These vegetables are classic pickling choices. If a vegetable looks less than fresh at the market, just omit it and add more of another.

VALUES ARE PER ½ CUP
FAT: 0G/0%
CALORIES: 93
SATURATED FAT: 0G
CARBOHYDRATE: 24G
PROTEIN: 2G
CHOLESTEROL: 0MG
SODIUM: 155MG

This vivid mix of vegetables reflects the bright spirit of the holiday season. Cover the tops of the jars with colored fabric and tie with pieces of raffia (rough twine) for a country touch. Include an attractively hand-lettered card describing some serving ideas—as part of an antipasto plate; as a side relish with roast meats; or as a condiment with grilled sandwiches.

Apple-Pear Sauce

Makes: 3 pints
Working time: 30 minutes
Total time: 1 hour plus cooling time

2½ pounds Granny Smith apples, peeled, cored, and quartered

2½ pounds ripe Bosc pears, peeled, cored, and quartered

2 cups apple juice

1 teaspoon grated lemon zest

½ cup firmly packed dark brown sugar

2 teaspoons cinnamon

1 teaspoon ground ginger

½ teaspoon ground allspice

1. Wash 3 pint jars and lids in hot soapy water and rinse well. Keep the lids and bands in hot water. To sterilize, place the jars, right-side up, on the rack in a water bath canner (or in a large saucepan), cover with hot water by 1 inch, and then boil for 10 minutes. Keep the jars in the hot water until ready to use.

2. In a large saucepan, combine the apples, pears, apple juice, and lemon zest. Bring to a boil over medium-high heat. Cover, reduce the heat to medium, and cook, stirring occasionally, until the apples and pears are tender, about 20 minutes.

3. In a blender or food processor, combine the apple-pear mixture, brown sugar, cinnamon, ginger, and allspice and purée until smooth. Return the mixture to the saucepan and cook over medium-low heat until the mixture is thickened, 5 to 10 minutes.

4. Drain the sterilized jars. Ladle the sauce through a sterilized funnel into the jars up to ¼ inch from the top, seal the jars, and refrigerate for up to 3 weeks. For longer storage, or if planning to keep unrefrigerated, process the filled jars in a boiling water bath for 10 minutes (p. 10).

Helpful hint: Any tart, juicy apple, such as Empire or McIntosh, would work well in this recipe.

Values are per ½ cup
Fat: 0.7g/0%
Calories: 153
Saturated Fat: 0.1g
Carbohydrate: 39g
Protein: 1g
Cholesterol: 0mg
Sodium: 5mg

Homemade applesauce—so simple to prepare, but always a welcome gift. This extra-special version combines tart Granny Smiths and sweet Bosc pears with cinnamon, ginger, and allspice for fragrance. We like this as a condiment for roasted meats, with French toast for a holiday brunch, or even as a dessert with a dollop of nonfat sour cream.

CHOCOLATE TRUFFLES

MAKES: 3 DOZEN
WORKING TIME: 20 MINUTES
TOTAL TIME: 45 MINUTES PLUS CHILLING TIME

Who would ever guess these delectable chocolate morsels are low in fat? And that mashed potatoes are the secret? The potatoes replicate the creamy-smooth texture of a truffle remarkably well, but without the fat. Place the truffles in pretty paper or gold foil cups, and pack them in a gift box along with a bottle of Champagne.

¾ pound baking potatoes (about 2), peeled and thinly sliced

1⅔ cups plus 1 tablespoon confectioners' sugar

⅔ cup plus 2 tablespoons unsweetened cocoa powder, preferably Dutch process

1 ounce semisweet chocolate, coarsely chopped

2 teaspoons unsalted butter

1 tablespoon orange liqueur

1 teaspoon vanilla

⅛ teaspoon salt

1. In a large saucepan of boiling water, cook the potatoes until tender, about 20 minutes. Drain well and return to the pan. With a potato masher or an electric beater, mash the potatoes until very smooth. Stir in 1⅔ cups of the confectioners' sugar, ⅔ cup of the cocoa, the chocolate, and butter. Cook over low heat, stirring constantly, until the mixture leaves the sides of the pan, about 4 minutes.

2. In a food processor, combine the potato mixture, liqueur, vanilla, and salt and process until smooth, about 2 minutes. Transfer to a bowl, cover with plastic wrap, and refrigerate until the mixture is firm enough to roll into balls, at least 3 hours or overnight.

3. With dampened hands, roll the truffle mixture into walnut-size balls. In a small bowl, stir together the remaining 1 tablespoon confectioners' sugar and remaining 2 tablespoons cocoa. Roll the truffles in the cocoa mixture, place in paper candy cups, and refrigerate for up to 5 days.

Helpful hints: Experiment with other flavored liqueurs, such as raspberry or hazelnut. Give the truffles as a gift soon after preparing, along with instructions to keep them refrigerated. The truffles may be rolled in additional cocoa just before serving, if desired.

VALUES ARE PER TRUFFLE
FAT: 1G/16%
CALORIES: 40
SATURATED FAT: 0.4G
CARBOHYDRATE: 9G
PROTEIN: 1G
CHOLESTEROL: 1MG
SODIUM: 9MG

Corn Relish

MAKES: 4 HALF-PINTS
WORKING TIME: 25 MINUTES
TOTAL TIME: 25 MINUTES

4 cups frozen corn kernels

1 cup cider vinegar

⅔ cup golden raisins

¼ cup firmly packed dark brown sugar

1 teaspoon chili powder

½ teaspoon salt

⅛ teaspoon cayenne pepper

Half red bell pepper, cut into ¼-inch dice

Half green bell pepper, cut into ¼-inch dice

2 tablespoons minced fresh cilantro

2 scallions, thinly sliced

1. Wash 4 half-pint jars and lids in hot soapy water and rinse well. Keep the lids and bands in hot water. To sterilize, place the jars, right-side up, on the rack in a water bath canner (or in a large saucepan), cover with hot water by 1 inch, and then boil for 10 minutes. Keep the jars in the hot water until ready to use.

2. In a large nonaluminum saucepan, combine the corn, vinegar, raisins, brown sugar, chili powder, salt, and cayenne. Bring to a boil over medium-high heat. Reduce the heat to medium, add the bell peppers, and cook, stirring occasionally, until the liquid is partially absorbed, 8 to 10 minutes.

3. Remove the mixture from the heat and stir in the cilantro and scallions. Drain the sterilized jars. Ladle the relish through a sterilized funnel into the jars up to ½ inch from the top, seal the jars, and refrigerate for up to 3 weeks. For longer storage, or if planning to keep unrefrigerated, process the filled jars in a boiling water bath for 15 minutes (p. 10).

Helpful hints: Fresh corn can be used instead of the frozen—you'll need about 8 ears to yield the right amount of kernels. If cilantro is not available, substitute flat-leaf Italian parsley.

VALUES ARE PER ¼ CUP
FAT: 0.4G/0%
CALORIES: 72
SATURATED FAT: 0G
CARBOHYDRATE: 18G
PROTEIN: 2G
CHOLESTEROL: 0MG
SODIUM: 74MG

We give this New England favorite our own flavor twist with raisins and cilantro—a touch of sunshine during the cold winter months. Wrap the jars in fabric or in sheets of colored cellophane and tie with strands of raffia or with ribbon for gift-giving. Serve as a robust condiment with roasted meats, as a sandwich topping, or even mixed with plain nonfat yogurt as a snack.

FLAVORED VINEGARS

MAKES: 2 QUARTS (PER FLAVOR)
WORKING TIME: 20 MINUTES (PER FLAVOR)
TOTAL TIME: 20 MINUTES PLUS STEEPING TIME

Herbed Shallot Vinegar

¾ cup sliced shallots
¼ cup sprigs of fresh rosemary
¼ cup sprigs of fresh thyme
4 small fresh red chili peppers
2 quarts distilled white vinegar

Tarragon Vinegar

20 sprigs of fresh tarragon
2 quarts rice vinegar

Raspberry Vinegar

4 cups fresh raspberries
2 tablespoons sugar
2 quarts rice vinegar
4 teaspoons vanilla
Eight 3 x ½-inch strips of
orange zest

Wash canning bottles or decorative bottles (see the recipes) in hot soapy water and rinse well. To sterilize, place the bottles in a large saucepan, cover with hot water by 1 inch, and then boil for 10 minutes. Keep the bottles in hot water until ready to use; drain.

Herbed Shallot Vinegar: Divide the shallots, rosemary, and thyme among 4 sterilized 2-cup (½-liter) canning bottles or decorative bottles. Place 1 chili in each bottle. In a medium nonaluminum saucepan, bring the vinegar to a boil. Pour the hot vinegar over the herb mixture, seal the bottles, and let stand for 2 weeks.

Tarragon Vinegar: Divide the tarragon among 4 sterilized 2-cup (½-liter) canning bottles or decorative bottles. In a medium nonaluminum saucepan, bring the vinegar to a boil. Pour the hot vinegar over the tarragon, seal the bottles, and let stand for 2 weeks.

Raspberry Vinegar: In a large bowl, stir together the raspberries and sugar. Divide the raspberry mixture among 2 sterilized 5-cup decorative bottles (or several smaller bottles to equal 10 cups). In a medium nonaluminum saucepan, bring the vinegar to a boil. Remove from the heat, stir in the vanilla, and pour over the berries. Divide the zest among the bottles, seal, and let stand for 2 weeks.

Helpful hints: Refrigerate the raspberry vinegar after opening; store the other vinegars in a cool cupboard. They will keep for at least 6 months.

VALUES ARE PER ¼ CUP
FAT: 0G/0%
CALORIES: <20
SATURATED FAT: 0G
CARBOHYDRATE: <6G
PROTEIN: 0G
CHOLESTEROL: 0MG
SODIUM: <1MG

Our three gourmet vinegars make fantastic gifts. What's more, they're surprisingly easy to prepare. Use these for the obvious—mixing up salad dressings. But don't stop there—sprinkle them over cooked vegetables, use in marinades for poultry, meat, and fish, and even drizzle over fresh fruit for an intriguing dessert.

Pumpkin Bread

Makes: 3 mini-loaves
Working time: 20 minutes
Total time: 1 hour 10 minutes plus cooling time

This fragrant quick bread tastes deceptively rich— buttermilk and reduced-fat sour cream are the secrets. Pack the loaf in its baking pan, if desired, and include the recipe for inspiration. As an added treat, toss in a bundle of cinnamon sticks, tied with ribbon, for making mulled cider to enjoy with the bread.

1½ cups flour

½ cup yellow cornmeal

1½ teaspoons baking powder

¾ teaspoon salt

¾ teaspoon cinnamon

½ teaspoon baking soda

½ teaspoon ground ginger

⅛ teaspoon ground cloves

⅛ teaspoon ground allspice

1 whole egg

2 egg whites

1 cup canned solid-pack pumpkin purée

1 cup low-fat (1.5%) buttermilk

⅔ cup firmly packed light brown sugar

½ cup reduced-fat sour cream

½ cup coarsely chopped pecans, toasted

1. Preheat the oven to 350°. Spray three 5½ x 3-inch mini-loaf pans with nonstick cooking spray. Dust with flour, shaking off the excess. In a large bowl, stir together the flour, cornmeal, baking powder, salt, cinnamon, baking soda, ginger, cloves, and allspice.

2. In a large bowl, with an electric mixer, beat together the egg, egg whites, pumpkin, buttermilk, brown sugar, and sour cream until well combined. Make a well in the center of the flour mixture and stir in the pumpkin mixture until just combined. Stir in the pecans.

3. Divide the batter among the prepared pans and bake for 50 minutes, or until a toothpick inserted in the center comes out just clean. Transfer to a wire rack and cool the loaves in the pans for 10 minutes. Turn out onto the rack and cool completely.

Helpful hints: Walnuts can be substituted for the pecans. If you'd like to bake a big batch of loaves for more extensive gift-giving, repeat the recipe as many times as you wish, rather than just increasing the amounts of the ingredients. These loaves can be tightly wrapped in plastic wrap and frozen for up to 3 months.

Values are per ½-inch slice
Fat: 2g/25%
Calories: 72
Saturated Fat: 0.4g
Carbohydrate: 12g
Protein: 2g
Cholesterol: 8mg
Sodium: 102mg

T hese "twice-baked" cookies— that's what biscotti means—include a flavorful combination of nuts, dried apricots, cornmeal, and a hint of crystallized ginger. For gift-giving, present them in decorative cookie tins or packaged in colored cellophane. Serve with coffee or espresso for dunking or, for added extravagance, with a glass of Champagne.

ALMOND-APRICOT BISCOTTI

MAKES: 4 DOZEN
WORKING TIME: 25 MINUTES
TOTAL TIME: 1 HOUR 15 MINUTES PLUS COOLING TIME

2¼ cups flour

¾ cup yellow cornmeal

⅓ cup sliced almonds, toasted and chopped

¼ cup finely chopped dried apricots

¼ cup cornstarch

1½ teaspoons baking powder

¼ teaspoon salt

1 whole egg

2 egg whites

1 cup firmly packed light brown sugar

3 tablespoons light olive oil or vegetable oil

1 tablespoon finely chopped crystallized ginger

1 teaspoon vanilla

½ teaspoon almond extract

1. Preheat the oven to 350°. Spray a baking sheet with nonstick cooking spray. In a medium bowl, stir together the flour, cornmeal, almonds, apricots, cornstarch, baking powder, and salt. In a large bowl, with an electric mixer, beat the egg, egg whites, brown sugar, oil, ginger, vanilla, and almond extract until creamy. Stir in the flour mixture just until the dough comes together.

2. Divide the dough in half. Roll each half into a 12-inch log (see tip; top photo), then flatten slightly so each log is 2 inches wide. Place the logs, 5 inches apart, on the prepared baking sheet and bake for 30 minutes, or until golden. Transfer to a wire rack and cool for 10 minutes. Leave the oven on. Transfer the logs to a work surface. With a serrated knife, slice the logs on the diagonal into generous ¼-inch-thick slices (bottom photo).

3. Place the slices on 2 ungreased baking sheets and bake for 7 minutes. Turn the cookies and bake for 8 minutes longer, or until crisp and lightly golden. Transfer to wire racks and cool completely.

Helpful hints: You can substitute pecans or hazelnuts for the almonds, and dried cherries or cranberries for the apricots. If the dough is too sticky to roll into logs, very lightly flour your hands and try again. Store the biscotti in an airtight container at room temperature for up to 3 weeks.

VALUES ARE PER COOKIE
FAT: 1G/19%
CALORIES: 66
SATURATED FAT: 0.2G
CARBOHYDRATE: 12G
PROTEIN: 1G
CHOLESTEROL: 4MG
SODIUM: 32MG

TIP

Roll each half of the dough into a 12-inch log, flatten slightly, and then place the logs, 5 inches apart, on the baking sheet—they will expand during baking. Slice the baked logs diagonally into generous ¼-inch-thick slices, and then return them to the oven for the final baking.

CRANBERRY SAUCE

MAKES: 5 HALF-PINTS
WORKING TIME: 20 MINUTES
TOTAL TIME: 20 MINUTES

Two 12-ounce packages fresh or frozen cranberries

2 cups orange juice

1¼ cups sugar

1 vanilla bean, split, or 2 teaspoons vanilla extract

1 teaspoon grated lime zest

½ teaspoon ground cloves

½ teaspoon ground ginger

1. Wash 5 half-pint jars and lids in hot soapy water and rinse well. Keep the lids and bands in hot water. To sterilize, place the jars, right-side up, on the rack in a water bath canner (or in a large saucepan), cover with hot water by 1 inch, and then boil for 10 minutes. Keep the jars in the hot water until ready to use.

2. In a large nonaluminum saucepan, stir together the cranberries, orange juice, sugar, vanilla bean (if using the vanilla extract, do not add it now), lime zest, cloves, and ginger. Bring to a boil over medium-high heat, reduce to a simmer, and cook, stirring occasionally, until some of the cranberries pop and the mixture is thickened, about 15 minutes.

3. Remove the mixture from the heat. Remove the vanilla bean and save it for another use. If using the vanilla extract, stir it into the mixture now. Drain the sterilized jars. Ladle the cranberry sauce through a sterilized funnel into the jars up to ¼ inch from the top, seal the jars, and refrigerate for up to 3 weeks. For longer storage, or if planning to keep unrefrigerated, process the filled jars in a boiling water bath for 15 minutes (p. 10).

Helpful hint: Frozen cranberries can be added directly to the saucepan—thawing is not needed.

VALUES ARE PER ¼ CUP
FAT: 0G/0%
CALORIES: 78
SATURATED FAT: 0G
CARBOHYDRATE: 20G
PROTEIN: 0G
CHOLESTEROL: 0MG
SODIUM: 1MG

Not just an ordinary cranberry sauce—we've added a mellow touch with vanilla. This is the ideal counterpoint for roast turkey or game birds. But do put its flavor to use in other ways—as a sandwich spread for a surprising twist, and for a snack, mix a little into plain nonfat yogurt.

Banana Bread

MAKES: 3 MINI-LOAVES
WORKING TIME: 25 MINUTES
TOTAL TIME: 1 HOUR 10 MINUTES PLUS COOLING TIME

⅔ cup golden raisins

3 tablespoons boiling water

2 tablespoons rum

2½ cups flour

1 teaspoon cinnamon

1 teaspoon baking powder

¾ teaspoon baking soda

½ teaspoon ground allspice

½ teaspoon salt

1 cup mashed bananas (about 3)

½ cup honey

½ cup low-fat (1.5%) buttermilk

2 tablespoons canola oil

½ cup chopped walnuts, toasted

1. Preheat the oven to 350°. Spray three 5½ x 3-inch mini-loaf pans with nonstick cooking spray. Dust with flour, shaking off the excess. In a small bowl, combine the raisins, boiling water, and rum and let stand for 10 minutes.

2. Meanwhile, in a medium bowl, stir together the flour, cinnamon, baking powder, baking soda, allspice, and salt. In a large bowl, stir together the bananas, honey, buttermilk, and oil. Drain the raisins, discarding the soaking liquid. Stir the drained raisins into the banana mixture along with the walnuts. Stir in the flour mixture until just combined.

3. Divide the batter among the prepared pans and bake for 45 minutes, or until a toothpick inserted in the center comes out clean. Transfer to a wire rack and cool the loaves in the pans for 10 minutes. Turn out onto the rack and cool completely.

Helpful hints: The riper the bananas, the more flavorful the bread. You can substitute pecans or almonds for the walnuts. If making several batches for gift-giving, repeat the recipe the appropriate number of times—don't just increase the amounts of the ingredients. The loaves will keep beautifully in the freezer for up to 3 months, wrapped tightly in plastic wrap to prevent freezer burn.

VALUES ARE PER ½-INCH SLICE
FAT: 2G/23%
CALORIES: 87
SATURATED FAT: 0.2G
CARBOHYDRATE: 16G
PROTEIN: 2G
CHOLESTEROL: 0MG
SODIUM: 79MG

We've loaded this quick bread with flavor—toasted walnuts, honey, buttermilk, spices, and, for a special touch, raisins plumped in rum. Wrap tightly in decorative foil and attach holiday stickers. This is marvelous spread with a little reduced-fat cream cheese and served with tea or coffee. Try toasting and topping it with all-fruit preserves for a tasty breakfast treat.

Double Chocolate Fudge Sauce

MAKES: 4 HALF-PINTS
WORKING TIME: 15 MINUTES
TOTAL TIME: 15 MINUTES

Semisweet chocolate and cocoa powder are the double flavor hits in this smooth, rich sauce. It's essential for spooning over holiday desserts— slices of angel food cake, poached pears or other fruit, a warm bread pudding, or anything else that begs for a delicious blanket of chocolate. Use the fudge sauce at room temperature or gently reheat.

8 ounces semisweet chocolate, coarsely chopped

1⅓ cups boiling water

½ cup light corn syrup

3 cups granulated sugar

1 cup firmly packed dark brown sugar

½ cup unsweetened cocoa powder, preferably Dutch process

¼ teaspoon salt

1 tablespoon vanilla

1. Wash 4 half-pint jars and lids in hot soapy water and rinse well. Keep the lids and bands in hot water. To sterilize, place the jars, right-side up, in a large saucepan, cover with hot water by 1 inch, and then boil for 10 minutes. Keep the jars in the hot water until ready to use.

2. In a medium saucepan, melt the chocolate over very low heat, stirring constantly. Stir in the boiling water and corn syrup. Add the granulated sugar, brown sugar, cocoa, and salt and stir well to combine. Cover, bring to a boil over medium heat, and cook without stirring for 3 minutes. Uncover and cook without stirring for 3 minutes longer.

3. Remove the mixture from the heat and stir in the vanilla. Drain the sterilized jars. Pour the fudge sauce into the jars, seal the jars, and refrigerate for up to 1 week. This sauce cannot be processed in a boiling water bath.

Helpful hint: For a mocha-flavored sauce, stir in a teaspoon of instant espresso powder with the vanilla.

VALUES ARE PER 1 TABLESPOON
FAT: 1G/14%
CALORIES: 76
SATURATED FAT: 0.7G
CARBOHYDRATE: 17G
PROTEIN: 0G
CHOLESTEROL: 0MG
SODIUM: 13MG

PINEAPPLE-MANGO CHUTNEY

MAKES: 4 HALF-PINTS
WORKING TIME: 25 MINUTES
TOTAL TIME: 25 MINUTES

20-ounce can crushed pineapple, drained

1 ripe mango, peeled and coarsely chopped

¾ cup coarsely chopped onion

⅔ cup golden raisins

⅔ cup cider vinegar

6 tablespoons firmly packed dark brown sugar

2 tablespoons chopped fresh ginger

2 cloves garlic, chopped

½ teaspoon mustard seeds

¼ teaspoon cinnamon

¼ teaspoon red pepper flakes

½ cup diced red bell pepper

1. Wash 4 half-pint jars and lids in hot soapy water and rinse well. Keep the lids and bands in hot water. To sterilize, place the jars, right-side up, on the rack in a water bath canner (or in a large saucepan), cover with hot water by 1 inch, and then boil for 10 minutes. Keep the jars in the hot water until ready to use.

2. In a large nonaluminum saucepan, stir together the pineapple, mango, onion, raisins, vinegar, brown sugar, ginger, garlic, mustard seeds, cinnamon, and pepper flakes. Bring to a boil over medium-high heat, reduce the heat to medium, and cook, stirring frequently, until the mango and onion begin to soften, about 8 minutes.

3. Remove the mixture from the heat and stir in the bell pepper. Drain the sterilized jars. Ladle the chutney through a sterilized funnel into the jars up to ¼ inch from the top, seal the jars, and refrigerate for up to 3 weeks. For longer storage, or if planning to keep unrefrigerated, process the filled jars in a boiling water bath for 10 minutes (p. 10).

Helpful hint: If mango is not available, substitute 2 large ripe peaches or nectarines.

VALUES ARE PER ¼ CUP
FAT: 0.1G/0%
CALORIES: 74
SATURATED FAT: 0G
CARBOHYDRATE: 19G
PROTEIN: 1G
CHOLESTEROL: 0MG
SODIUM: 4MG

This classic combination of sweet-tart flavors is easily put together at home and makes an intriguing gift. Typically served as a refreshing condiment with curries, chutney is also excellent as an accompaniment to roast meats, as a sandwich spread, or with eggs for a brunch. Package in glass canning jars, and attach a recipe for a favorite chicken curry.

GLOSSARY

Allspice—A dark, round, dried berry about the size of a peppercorn, called allspice because it tastes like a blend of cloves, cinnamon, and nutmeg. Usually sold in ground form, allspice is often mistakenly thought to be a mix of several spices.

Almond—The seed of the sweet almond tree, commonly sold whole, slivered, or sliced. Whole and sliced almonds come both natural (with skin) and blanched (without skin); slivered almonds are always blanched. Use almonds sparingly since nuts add fat. Store in the freezer for up to 1 year.

Apple, Granny Smith—A crisp, juicy apple that is imported from New Zealand and Australia, and also is cultivated in this country. Speckled green in color and sweet-tart in flavor, this apple is excellent for cooking and eating out of hand.

Apricot, dried—A dried fruit that is intensely flavored with the essence of the apricot, perfect for low-fat cooking since its tartness compensates for the absence of flavorful fat. Some dried apricots are treated with sulfur dioxide to preserve their color; the unsulfured variety is darker in color and richer in flavor. To plump dried apricots, soak them in warm water, orange juice, or brandy.

Baking powder—An essential leavening agent for quick breads and other nonyeast-risen baked goods. When mixed with a liquid, it releases the gas carbon dioxide, which causes airiness, or rising. Double-acting baking powder is the most common form—a little gas is released when the batter is moistened; more is released during baking. Always check the expiration date before using. To test for potency, dissolve a little baking powder in warm water—it should bubble.

Baking soda—A leavening agent that is often used in combination with baking powder when there is an acid ingredient such as buttermilk. Both baking powder and baking soda are usually mixed first with the other dry ingredients in the recipe because as soon they are moistened, they immediately begin to react, releasing carbon dioxide, which causes the rising.

Brandy—A liquor distilled from wine or fermented fruit juices, such as peach or apple. Traditionally savored in snifters after a fine meal, brandy is also used in cooking, especially in sauces for meats, and in all kinds of holiday baking. Brandy is usually aged in wood casks, which contributes to its intense flavor—a little goes a long way.

Buttermilk—A milk product made by adding a special bacterial culture to nonfat or low-fat milk. Buttermilk lends a tangy taste, a slightly thickened texture, and a subtle richness to baked goods such as quick breads and cookies, without significant fat. Use within 1 week of purchase. In a pinch, make your own "buttermilk" by combining 1 tablespoon lemon juice or vinegar with enough milk to make 1 cup.

Caper—The flower bud of a small bush found in Mediterranean countries. To make capers, the buds are dried and then pickled in vinegar with some salt—to reduce saltiness, rinse before using. The piquant taste of capers permeates any sauce quickly, and only a scant few are needed for the flavor boost.

Cardamom—An aromatic spice that belongs to the ginger family. Popularly used in curries, cardamom imparts a sweet flavor in cooking, and is frequently used in baking as well, especially in Scandinavian specialties. It is available ground or in whole seeds, and even as pods that contain the seeds. Once ground, the seeds begin to lose their flavor potency.

Chestnut—The fruit of the chestnut tree, well known as a favorite for roasting and serving at holiday time. Chestnuts can also be boiled, preserved, and candied. Their sweet flavor and crumbly texture complement turkey and other game birds, and they are delicious in a variety of desserts. If buying whole nuts, make sure they are plump and unblemished, and store in a cool spot. Chestnuts are also available canned—whole, in pieces, or as a purée.

Chocolate, semisweet—A blend of unsweetened chocolate, cocoa butter, and sugar, commonly used in baking and for creating such treats as dessert sauces. Store in a cool, dry place, tightly wrapped to protect it from moisture. If kept in too warm a spot, chocolate may develop a grayish coating, which doesn't affect the flavor or melting properties. Bittersweet (not unsweetened) chocolate can be substituted.

Clam juice, bottled—A convenient form of clam juice. It adds a briny flavor wherever it is used; in soups and stews—even a sprinkling in oyster stuffings adds a special touch. If using canned clams or oysters rather than fresh, the addition of bottled clam juice intensifies the seafood flavor.

Cornmeal, yellow—A flour-like, finely textured product made from ground dried corn kernels. Yellow cornmeal is the most readily available form, but white and blue varieties make an intriguing change. Cornmeal adds a pleasant crunch and mild sweetness to breads, biscuits, cakes, cookies, and even pie crusts. It can also be baked and served as a creamy side dish, as in the classic Southern spoonbread.

Cottage cheese—A tangy, spoonable cheese, available in creamed (highest in fat) and dry-curd styles. Low-fat versions of cottage cheese work well in cheesecakes and similar cakes to keep them nutritionally sensible. Cottage cheese is perishable and should be used within a week of purchase.

Cocoa powder, unsweetened—Pure chocolate from which most of the cocoa butter has been pressed. Cocoa is a boon to low-fat dessert making since it is reasonably low in fat. The Dutch version is treated with alkali, which darkens the color and imparts a rich chocolate flavor.

Cranberry—A small, tart, firm berry that is essential to American holiday cooking. Cranberries are at their peak from September to December, but you can stock up and freeze them for up to 1 year. Frozen cranberries can often be added to a recipe without thawing. Cranberries are served cooked and sweetened as a relish accompanying roast turkey, as well as in pie fillings, cakes, and even stuffings.

Cream cheese, reduced-fat—A light cream cheese, commonly called Neufchâtel, with about one-third less fat than regular cream cheese. It can be used as a substitute for regular cream cheese. A small amount used in baking or in sauces duplicates the richness of full-fat cheese or heavy cream.

Cream of tartar—A white, powdery natural fruit acid that is a by-product of winemaking. Cream of tartar is invaluable for increasing the volume and stability of beaten egg whites. Also, when combined with baking soda, it releases carbon dioxide to lighten batters.

Currants, dried—Tiny raisins made from a small variety of grape. Use interchangeably with raisins for baking or in sauces or rice dishes, keeping in mind that currants are smaller and will disperse more flavor and sweetness because you get more currants in every bite.

Endive, Belgian—A bullet-shaped member of the chicory family with a pleasing bitter taste; its individual spears or leaves make wonderful "boats" for appetizer dips. Select small, firm heads that are creamy white with yellowish tips. Refrigerate in damp paper towels in a perforated plastic bag for no more than 2 days.

Evaporated milk, skimmed and low-fat—Canned, unsweetened, homogenized milk that has had more than half of its fat removed: In the skimmed version, 100 percent of the fat has been removed; the low-fat version contains 1 percent fat. Used in baking or cooking, it adds a creamy richness with almost no fat. Store at room temperature for up to 6 months until opened, then refrigerate for up to 1 week.

Flour, cake—A type of flour milled from soft wheat, and thus lower in gluten. This is an excellent choice for baking delicate cakes since it gives them a fine-textured, tender crumb. If you need to substitute regular all-purpose flour, place 2 tablespoons cornstarch in a 1-cup dry measure and spoon in enough all-purpose flour to equal 1 level cup.

Gelatin, unflavored—A powder containing animal protein, used to thicken and set various preparations. Gelatin is ideal in desserts, especially low-fat renditions of favorites such as chiffon pies and cheesecakes, and in fruit glazes for cakes and pies. For best results, always dissolve the gelatin in cold water before adding it to a hot liquid. Certain fresh fruits, such as pineapple, kiwi, and papaya, contain an enzyme that prevents the gelatin from gelling.

Ginger, crystallized—A confection made from fresh ginger that has been chopped into coarse pieces, cooked in syrup, and then coated in sugar. Sweet-hot in flavor, it is used in baking, as a garnish for desserts, and in spicy condiments and sauces. Look for it in jars in the spice section of the supermarket.

Grapes, seedless—Small vine-growing fruits, available all year round but at their most plentiful from late summer through early winter. They make a colorful, fat-free addition to winter fruit salads as well as many other desserts. Select grapes that are plump, vibrantly colored, and firmly attached to the stem. Refrigerate, unwashed, loosely wrapped in paper towels in a plastic bag.

Hazelnut—A sweet, richly flavored nut that can substitute for practically any nut in a dessert. Beware of the fat, however, and use judiciously. Refrigerate shelled hazelnuts for up to 6 months. If the nuts are unblanched, with the papery brown skin still intact, toast them in a 350° oven for 5 to 7 minutes. Then rub off the skins with a kitchen towel.

Honey—A sweet, sticky substance made by honey bees from flower nectar. It ranges in flavor from mild (orange blossom) to very strong (buckwheat). Deliciously versatile, honey can sweeten savory dishes such as glazed carrots, add interest to dressings for fruit salads, and enrich baked goods such as cakes and even crusts for pies and cheesecakes. Store honey at room temperature. If it crystallizes, place the jar in a pan of warm (not hot) water, until the honey becomes liquid.

Kasha—A Russian word that has become the familiar supermarket term for roasted buckwheat kernels. Nutty in flavor, kasha is sold in whole grain, coarse-, medium-, and fine-ground versions. Store kasha in the refrigerator for up to 6 months, or in the freezer for up to 1 year.

Marjoram—A member of the mint family that tastes like mildly sweet oregano. Fresh marjoram should be added at the end of the cooking so the flavor doesn't vanish. Dried marjoram, sold in leaf and ground form (the more intense leaf being preferable), stands up to longer cooking.

Molasses—A by-product from the refining of sugarcane or sugar beets. Molasses is available in two forms: Light molasses is commonly used as a syrup for pancakes and waffles; dark molasses, which is less sweet and thicker, is used to sweeten and flavor hearty baked goods, such as gingerbread. Store in a cool, dry place.

Mustard seeds—The whole seeds of the mustard plant. Ranging in color from white to black with a whole spectrum of yellow in between, mustard seeds vary in strength from mild to hot. Use them to boost the flavor of salad dressings, curries, and chutneys.

Nutmeg—The hard, brown seed of the nutmeg tree. The whole spice lasts almost indefinitely, and you can grate it freshly as needed on a special grater or on an ordinary box grater to add a sweet, nutty spiciness to desserts, sauces, and savory dishes. Ground nutmeg offers about the same flavor but with less pungency.

Onion, pearl—A tiny, mild-flavored onion, about ½ inch in diameter. Pearl onions are favored in stews, soups, and saucy sautés for their crunchy texture and attractively small size. A bag of the frozen variety is a fine substitute for fresh.

Pear, Bartlett—A sweet, fine-textured, bell-shaped pear that turns yellow when ripe; delicious for eating out of hand and cooking, especially poaching. Let ripen at room temperature, then refrigerate for no more than 3 or 4 days. For baking and cooking, the pear should be firm and slightly underripe.

Pecan—A native American nut that is equally at home in pies and quick breads. Since pecans have the highest fat content of any nut, they are the most perishable and should be stored in the refrigerator for up to 3 months, or in the freezer for up to 6 months.

Pumpkin, canned—An excellent "substitute" ingredient in baking, especially when there is no time to roast and purée a fresh pumpkin. Buy the solid-pack pumpkin purée, not the sweetened pie filling. Pumpkin pie is the obvious use, but the purée is also delicious in soups, quick breads, and cakes.

Oats, rolled—A chewy-textured grain that adds a nutty taste to cookies, cakes, and other baked desserts. Old-fashioned rolled oats are made from oat groats (the whole kernels) that have been hulled, then steamed and flattened. Quick-cooking oats are made in the same manner, but from cut groats.

Poppy seeds—The tiny, bluish-black seeds of the poppy plant. They add a nutty crunch to cakes, breads, and many noodle dishes. Dark, shiny color indicates freshness. Store in the freezer for up to 6 months.

Rum, dark—A liquor distilled from fermented sugarcane or molasses. Just a little adds flavorful depth to a variety of baked desserts, especially chocolate cakes. Orange juice can often be substituted, although the flavor will be different.

Sour cream—A soured dairy product, resulting from treating sweet cream with a lactic acid culture. Regular sour cream contains at least 18 percent milk fat; reduced-fat sour cream contains 4 percent fat; nonfat sour cream contains no fat. In cooking, the reduced-fat version can be substituted for regular sour cream; use the nonfat cautiously since it behaves differently, especially in baking. To avoid curdling, do not subject sour cream to high heat.

Sugar, confectioners'—Granulated white sugar that has been crushed to a powder; a little cornstarch is usually mixed in to prevent caking. The most common form is 10X or ultrafine. Since this sugar dissolves so readily, it is often used in icings and glazes. It is also familiar as a finishing touch for unfrosted cakes and other desserts.

Sugar, brown—A mix of granulated white sugar and molasses with a softer texture than regular white sugar. Dark brown sugar has more molasses than light, and as a result has a richer, sweeter flavor, although the two can be used interchangeably in recipes. To soften brown sugar, tuck an apple

slice in the box and seal tightly for a day or two.

Toasting—A simple technique to enhance the flavor of nuts, making them taste richer. All kinds of desserts, including cakes and cookies, as well as salads benefit from their addition. Spread the nuts on a baking sheet with sides and bake at 350° for 8 to 10 minutes, stirring occasionally.

Vanilla bean—The dried pod of a climbing orchid, imported from various parts of the world. Vanilla is a given in many desserts, especially those with chocolate, for which it has a special affinity. The whole vanilla bean can be simmered in liquids such as milk for custards, or the pod can be split and the seeds scraped into a batter or other mixture. To reuse the bean after cooking, rinse, blot dry, wrap in plastic wrap, and store at room temperature to be used a few more times. After that, tuck it into a sugar canister to make vanilla sugar. Pure vanilla extract is a convenient substitute—but avoid imitation vanilla, which has a bitter, chemical aftertaste.

Wild rice—Not a true rice but an aquatic grass seed with a long, dark brown kernel and a nutty, earthy flavor. It is deliciously suited for stuffings and dressings for turkey and game. Traditionally harvested by hand from shallow lakes in the northern central region of the U.S. and in Canada, wild rice is now also cultivated in paddies and harvested by machine.

Zest, citrus—The very thin, outermost colored part of the rind of a lemon, lime, or orange that contains strongly flavored oils. Citrus zest imparts an intense flavor that helps to compensate for the lack of flavorful fat, and is especially welcome in baked goods, including cakes and cookies. Remove the zest with a grater, citrus zester, or vegetable peeler.

INDEX

Time-Life Books is a division of Time Life Inc.

PRESIDENT and CEO: John M. Fahey Jr.

TIME-LIFE BOOKS

MANAGING EDITOR: Roberta Conlan

Director of Design: Michael Hentges
Editorial Production Manager: Ellen Robling
Senior Editors: Russell B. Adams Jr., Janet Cave, Lee Hassig,
    Robert Somerville, Henry Woodhead
Special Projects Editor: Rita Thievon Mullin
Director of Operations: Eileen Bradley
Director of Photography and Research: John Conrad Weiser
Library: Louise D. Forstall

PRESIDENT: John D. Hall

Vice President, Director of New Product Development: Neil Kagan
Associate Director, New Product Development: Quentin S. McAndrew
Marketing Director, New Product Development: Robin B. Shuster
Vice President, Book Production: Marjann Caldwell
Production Manager: Marlene Zack
Consulting Editor: Catherine Boland Hackett

Design for Great Taste–Low Fat by David Fridberg of
Miles Fridberg Molinaroli, Inc.

REBUS, INC.
PUBLISHER: Rodney M. Friedman
EDITORIAL DIRECTOR: Charles L. Mee

Editorial Staff for *Holiday Cooking*
Director, Recipe Development and Photography: Grace Young
Editorial Director: Kate Slate
Senior Recipe Developer: Sandra Rose Gluck
Recipe Developers: Amanda Cushman, Helen Jones, Paul Piccuito
Managing Editor: Janet Charatan
Associate Editor: Julee Binder
Writer: David J. Ricketts
Nutritionists: Hill Nutrition Associates

Art Directors: Sara Bowman, Timothy Jeffs
Senior Production Editor: Susan Paige
Photographers: Lisa Koenig, Vincent Lee, Lars Lönninge
Photographers' Assistants: Katie Bleacher, Eugene De Lucie,
    Robert Presciutti, Thomas Skovende
Food Stylists: A.J. Battifarano, Karen Pickus, Karen Tack,
    Andrea Swensen
Assistant Food Stylists: Mako Antonishek, Catherine Chatham,
    Amy Lord, Ellie Ritt
Prop Stylist: Debrah Donahue
Prop Coordinator: Karin Martin

Cover dishes courtesy of Wedgwood

Library of Congress Cataloging-in-Publication Data

Holiday cooking.
p. cm. -- (Great taste, low fat)
Includes index.
ISBN 0-7835-4553-3 (alk. paper)
1. Holiday cookery. 2. Low-fat diet--Recipes. 3. Quick and easy
cookery. I. Time-Life Books. II. Series.
TX739.H6518 1995
641.5'68--dc20
95-38145
CIP

Other Publications
THE TIME-LIFE COMPLETE GARDENER
HOME REPAIR AND IMPROVEMENT
JOURNEY THROUGH THE MIND AND BODY
WEIGHT WATCHERS® SMART CHOICE RECIPE COLLECTION
TRUE CRIME
THE AMERICAN INDIANS
THE ART OF WOODWORKING
LOST CIVILIZATIONS
ECHOES OF GLORY
THE NEW FACE OF WAR
HOW THINGS WORK
WINGS OF WAR
CREATIVE EVERYDAY COOKING
COLLECTOR'S LIBRARY OF THE UNKNOWN
CLASSICS OF WORLD WAR II
TIME-LIFE LIBRARY OF CURIOUS AND UNUSUAL FACTS
AMERICAN COUNTRY
VOYAGE THROUGH THE UNIVERSE
THE THIRD REICH
MYSTERIES OF THE UNKNOWN
TIME FRAME
FIX IT YOURSELF
FITNESS, HEALTH & NUTRITION
SUCCESSFUL PARENTING
HEALTHY HOME COOKING
UNDERSTANDING COMPUTERS
LIBRARY OF NATIONS
THE ENCHANTED WORLD
THE KODAK LIBRARY OF CREATIVE PHOTOGRAPHY
GREAT MEALS IN MINUTES
THE CIVIL WAR
PLANET EARTH
COLLECTOR'S LIBRARY OF THE CIVIL WAR
THE EPIC OF FLIGHT
THE GOOD COOK
WORLD WAR II
THE OLD WEST

*For information on and a full description of any of the Time-Life Books series
listed above, please call 1-800-621-7026 or write:*
Reader Information
Time-Life Customer Service
P.O. Box C-32068
Richmond, Virginia 23261-2068

METRIC CONVERSION CHARTS

VOLUME EQUIVALENTS
(fluid ounces/milliliters and liters)

US	Metric
1 tsp	5 ml
1 tbsp (½ fl oz)	15 ml
¼ cup (2 fl oz)	60 ml
⅓ cup	80 ml
½ cup (4 fl oz)	120 ml
⅔ cup	160 ml
¾ cup (6 fl oz)	180 ml
1 cup (8 fl oz)	240 ml
1 qt (32 fl oz)	950 ml
1 qt + 3 tbsps	1 L
1 gal (128 fl oz)	4 L

Conversion formula
Fluid ounces X 30 = milliliters
1000 milliliters = 1 liter

WEIGHT EQUIVALENTS
(ounces and pounds/grams and kilograms)

US	Metric
¼ oz	7 g
½ oz	15 g
¾ oz	20 g
1 oz	30 g
8 oz (½ lb)	225 g
12 oz (¾ lb)	340 g
16 oz (1 lb)	455 g
35 oz (2.2 lbs)	1 kg

Conversion formula
Ounces X 28.35 = grams
1000 grams = 1 kilogram

LINEAR EQUIVALENTS
(inches and feet/centimeters and meters)

US	Metric
¼ in	.75 cm
½ in	1.5 cm
¾ in	1 cm
1 in	2.5 cm
6 in	15 cm
12 in (1 ft)	30 cm
39 in	1 m

Conversion formula
Inches X 2.54 = centimeters
100 centimeters = 1 meter

TEMPERATURE EQUIVALENTS
(Fahrenheit/Celsius)

US	Metric
0° (freezer temperature)	-18°
32° (water freezes)	0°
98.6°	37°
180° (water simmers*)	82°
212° (water boils*)	100°
250° (low oven)	120°
350° (moderate oven)	175°
425° (hot oven)	220°
500° (very hot oven)	260°

*at sea level

Conversion formula
Degrees Fahrenheit minus
32 ÷ 1.8 = degrees Celsius